Decoding the TOEFL® iBT

Advanced

READING   Answers & Explanations

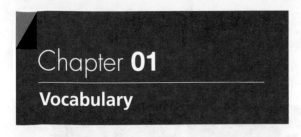

Chapter 01

Vocabulary

Practice with Short Passages   p. 16

A │ Nomadic Wanderings in Eurasia

Answers   1 Ⓑ   2 Ⓒ

Answer Explanations

1 Ⓑ Sustenance such as milk and meat is nourishment.

2 Ⓒ When the nomads clashed with people living in Europe, they fought with them.

Vocabulary

· **intermittent** = sporadic; happening off and on
· **livestock** = animals raised on farms
· **roam** = to wander
· **incursion** = an invasion

B │ The Origins of Black Holes

Answers   1 Ⓒ   2 Ⓐ

Answer Explanations

1 Ⓒ When a giant star exhausts its hydrogen and helium fuel through the course of nuclear reactions, it finishes using all of its fuel.

2 Ⓐ When time seems to slow to a standstill, it appears to halt.

Vocabulary

· **phenomenon** = something impressive or unusual
· **compressed** = condensed; pressed together
· **supernova** = a star that has exploded
· **gargantuan** = very large; huge

C │ Labor Market Immobility

Answers   1 Ⓓ   2 Ⓑ

Answer Explanations

1 Ⓓ Workers who get laid off are fired.

2 Ⓑ People who can overcome a handicap regarding work are able to overcome a disadvantage that they have.

Vocabulary

· **undesirable** = unwanted
· **commitment** = an obligation; a duty
· **switch** = to change
· **skill set** = all of the abilities a person has

Mapping

❶ employment   ❷ Geographical
❸ housing   ❹ Industrial
❺ skill sets (= skills) ❻ Occupational
❼ lawyers

Summary

❶ immobility   ❷ Geographical
❸ inability   ❹ Industrial
❺ skills   ❻ available
❼ Occupational   ❽ change

Practice with Long Passages   p. 20

A │ The Fiction of Jane Austen

Answers

1 Ⓐ   2 Ⓑ   3 Ⓐ   4 ①, ②, ④

Answer Explanations

1 Ⓐ When Jane Austen snubbed the conventional forms of literature of her day, she ignored them.

2 Ⓑ The author notes, "It was not until the 1900s, however, that her name attained worldwide fame."

3 Ⓐ There is no mention in either paragraph of which kinds of characters Jane Austen preferred to serve as the narrators of her stories.

4 ①, ②, ④ The summary sentence notes that Jane Austen wrote in a style that was unique to her and published several novels about morals and manners. These thoughts are best described in answer choices ①, ②, and ④. Answer choices ③ and ⑤ are minor points, so they are incorrect answers. And answer choice ⑥ is not mentioned in the passage, so it is wrong as well.

Vocabulary

· **circumstances** = a set of conditions
· **posthumously** = following one's death
· **anonymously** = with no name; unnamed
· **element** = an aspect or feature

B | Frog Calls

Answers

1 Ⓒ 2 Ⓒ 3 Ⓑ

4 Mating Call: ②, ④, ⑦ Warning Call: ①, ⑥
Release Call: ③, ⑨

Answer Explanations

1 Ⓒ The sentence points out that frog mating calls sound the same to humans, but female frogs can differentiate between them. This thought is best expressed by the sentence in answer choice Ⓒ.

2 Ⓒ The "it" that may release the frog is a predator.

3 Ⓑ When a male latches onto a female, he grasps the female.

4 Mating Call: ②, ④, ⑦
Warning Call: ①, ⑥
Release Call: ③, ⑨
Regarding mating calls, the passage reads, "The loudest, most forceful calls attract the most potential female mates," (②, ④) and, "Mating calls are among the most important of a male frog's repertoire. If he cannot successfully attract a mate, he cannot breed and pass on his genes to a new generation." (⑦) About warning calls, the author writes, "Warning calls are employed to alert other frogs of some nearby danger and are commonly heard when a predator ventures near," (①) and, "If a predator attacks a frog, it will make a distress call, which is high pitched—almost like a scream—and is intended to startle the predator. This distress call is almost always made when a predator succeeds in grabbing the frog because, should it be sufficiently surprised, it may release the frog, which might permit the animal to make its escape." (⑥) And as for release calls, it is written, "Females that have already mated may make this call when different male frogs grab hold of them," (③) and, "The final major call made by frogs is the release call, which is employed when another frog grabs it by mistake. This regularly happens during the mating season, when male frogs desperate for a mate unwittingly grab other males." (⑨)

Vocabulary

- **distinguish** = to tell the difference between
- **trespass** = to go on land belonging to another
- **aggressively** = hostilely
- **startle** = to shock; to surprise

iBT Practice Test p. 24

Answers

PASSAGE 1

1 Ⓑ 2 Ⓑ 3 Ⓒ 4 Ⓐ 5 Ⓑ
6 Ⓐ 7 Ⓓ 8 Ⓓ 9 ❷
10 ②, ③, ④

PASSAGE 2

11 Ⓒ 12 Ⓐ 13 Ⓓ 14 Ⓒ 15 Ⓑ
16 Ⓒ 17 Ⓓ 18 Ⓒ 19 ❶
20 ②, ④, ⑤

PASSAGE 1

Answer Explanations

1 Factual Information Question

Ⓑ The passage reads, "It was early in the fifteenth century that Italian architects were introduced to the ideas of humanism, which initiated the Renaissance, and they were also exposed to the works of ancient Roman architects that had been on display for all to see for more than a thousand years. They began making new designs, and this trend soon spread to other European countries, particularly France, Germany, England, and Russia."

2 Rhetorical Purpose Question

Ⓑ About the Gothic Age, the author writes, "Roman arches were semicircular as opposed to the more pointed arches used in the Gothic Age, which preceded the Renaissance." So the author is pointing out a difference between the architectural styles of the Gothic Age and the Renaissance.

3 Negative Factual Information Question

Ⓒ It is not true that Ionic, Doric, and Corinthian columns were used less often than Roman columns.

4 Vocabulary Question

Ⓐ Symmetrical façades are those which are balanced.

5 Sentence Simplification Question

Ⓑ The sentence points out that Renaissance architects designed religious buildings like they did in the Middle Ages and also designed other types of buildings. This thought is best expressed by the sentence in answer choice Ⓑ.

6 Factual Information Question

Ⓐ The author mentions, "Work on it had begun in 1296, but it was still incomplete in the early fifteenth century as the planned dome had not been constructed. Brunelleschi was commissioned to complete the project and, after considerable effort, successfully fulfilled his mission."

7 Inference Question

Ⓓ The passage reads, "He based most of the dome's construction on observations he had made of the dome of the Pantheon in Rome. While his dome utilized Roman engineering principles, it was not a true Roman dome as it had a pointed shape and used ribbed supports, much like those found in Gothic architecture." Since the dome of Florence Cathedral "was not a true Roman dome," the author implies that the dome of the Pantheon looks different from the dome of Florence Cathedral.

8 Vocabulary Question

Ⓓ When the new style of architecture was well underway, it was currently being developed.

9 Insert Text Question

② The sentence before the second square reads, "Considered the pinnacle of Renaissance architecture, it was designed by several architects, including Michelangelo." The sentence to be added starts with "He," which refers to Michelangelo. Therefore, the two sentences go well together.

10 Prose Summary Question

②, ③, ④ The summary sentence notes that the ancient Greeks and Romans influenced the architects of the Renaissance. This thought is best described in answer choices ②, ③, and ④. Answer choices ①, ⑤, and ⑥ are all minor points, so they are incorrect answers.

PASSAGE 2

Answer Explanations

11 Factual Information Question

Ⓒ The passage reads, "The palace was home to the rulers of France from the late seventeenth century until the onset of the French Revolution in 1789."

12 Vocabulary Question

Ⓐ When a mother is domineering, she is overbearing in how she behaves toward someone.

13 Inference Question

Ⓓ In writing, "During the early years of his reign, Louis was beset by various factions of individuals wishing to topple him from power and by wars both internal and external," the author implies that the reign of Louis XIII was not peaceful.

14 Rhetorical Purpose Question

Ⓒ About the Day of the Dupes, the author writes, "This came to a head on November 1630, when an event occurred called the Day of the Dupes because

those who thought they had succeeded actually lost. Marie obtained the support of numerous nobles due to their growing dislike of France's involvement in the costly Thirty Years' War. Marie secreted the king to her own Luxembourg Palace in Paris in order to influence him to remove Richelieu from power. Richelieu found them, and after a confrontation, Marie believed she had won the struggle. Louis subsequently fled to his hunting lodge in Versailles. After taking some time to reflect upon his rash decision, the next day, Louis summoned Richelieu to Versailles, reconciled with him, and banished his mother and her supporters from court life." The author describes this event to show how Cardinal Richelieu gained power in Louis's court.

15 Sentence Simplification Question

Ⓑ The sentence points out that Louis thought about his decision, made up with Richelieu, and then had his mother and her supporters leave Versailles. This thought is best expressed by the sentence in answer choice Ⓑ.

16 Vocabulary Question

Ⓒ When Louis became smitten with Versailles, it means that he liked it very much.

17 Inference Question

Ⓓ The author writes, "Louis XIV spent very much treasure and time making Versailles the envy of Europe by greatly expanding the main structures and by constructing lavish gardens and water fountains." In doing so, the author implies that Versailles became one of the most luxurious palaces in Europe.

18 Vocabulary Question

Ⓒ When buildings are hemmed in by a growing city, it means that they are constrained by the city and have nowhere to expand.

19 Insert Text Question

① The sentence before the first square reads, "It was essentially a showpiece designed to cow France's enemies and friends alike." The sentence to be added points out that people who visited the palace were intimidated—or cowed—by its size and beauty. Thus the two sentences go well together.

20 Prose Summary Question

②, ④, ⑤ The summary sentence notes that the palace at Versailles expanded in size and importance during the reigns of Louis XIII and Louis XIV. This thought is best described in answer choices ②, ④, and ⑤. Answer choice ⑥ is a minor point, so it is an incorrect answer. Answer choices ① and ③ contain information not mentioned in the passage, so they are also incorrect.

Vocabulary Review

p. 34

Answers

A
1 humble   2 circumstances
3 compressed   4 phenomenon
5 initiate

B
1 a   2 a   3 b   4 a   5 b
6 b   7 b   8 a   9 b   10 b

Chapter 02
Reference

Practice with Short Passages   p. 38

A | The Use of Light in Art Galleries

Answers   1 Ⓒ   2 Ⓑ

Answer Explanations

1 Ⓒ The "they" that are not fixed in place are recessed lights.

2 Ⓑ The "it" that should be placed where sunlight cannot directly hit it is artwork.

Vocabulary

• **embedded** = enclosed; sunken
• **ambient** = regarding the surrounding area
• **glare** = shine; brightness
• **mute** = to reduce the intensity of

B | Primates and Language

Answers   1 Ⓓ   2 Ⓓ

Answer Explanations

1 Ⓓ The "which" that represent human speech are lexigrams.

2 Ⓓ The "she" that scientists believe could actually understand English was Koko.

Vocabulary

• **primate** = animals such as humans, apes, and monkeys
• **concentrate** = to focus; to stress
• **skeptical** = doubtful
• **insightful** = perceptive

C | Animal Packs

Answers   1 Ⓒ   2 Ⓑ

Answer Explanations

1 Ⓒ The "they" that virtually always get first choice of any food acquired in addition to the largest portions are the alphas.

2 Ⓑ The "it" that exposes its belly is the omega.

Vocabulary

• **preferential** = favorable; showing preference to another
• **virtually** = nearly; almost
• **fawning** = affectionate; servile
• **confrontation** = a fight; hostility

Mapping

❶ packs   ❷ alpha
❸ strongest   ❹ preferential
❺ Beta   ❻ Omega
❼ subservient   ❽ threat

Summary

❶ predators   ❷ leaders
❸ alpha   ❹ first
❺ status   ❻ defeated
❼ challenge   ❽ weakest

Practice with Long Passages   p. 42

A | Adam Smith's Views on Economics

Answers

1 Ⓐ   2 Ⓒ   3 Ⓒ   4 ②, ⑤, ⑥

Answer Explanations

1 Ⓐ The passage reads, "His 1776 work *An Inquiry into the Nature and Causes of the Wealth of Nations*, more commonly shortened to *The Wealth of Nations*, has had an enormous influence on economic theory and policy from the time it was published to the present day. Smith is particularly noted for his argument that free market economies are superior to controlled economies as well as his

writing on the division of labor."

2 Ⓒ About Francis Hutchinson, the passage notes, "Smith's mentor, Francis Hutchinson, a professor at the University of Glasgow, had a major effect on Smith's career path and later writings. It was during Smith's tenure there that he began formulating his theories on economics which would later bring him worldwide fame." So the author mentions him to name him as an influence on Adam Smith's economic theories.

3 Ⓒ The "they" that could make a much larger number of pins in a single day were many workers.

4 ②, ⑤, ⑥ The summary sentence notes that Adam Smith is a noted modern economist known mostly for his work on free market economies and the division of labor. This thought is best described in answer choices ②, ⑤, and ⑥. Answer choice ① contains incorrect information, so it is a wrong answer. Answer choices ③ and ④ are minor points, so they are also incorrect.

Vocabulary

- **rhetoric** = the art of using language effectively
- **formulate** = to create; to make
- **benevolent** = kind
- **agrarian** = relating to the land

B | The Eliminating of Dams

Answers

| 1 Ⓓ | 2 Ⓓ | 3 Ⓑ | 4 ②, ④, ⑤ |

Answer Explanations

1 Ⓓ The "these" that combine to distort the characteristics of their rivers are large amounts of silt, gravel, plant matter, and other debris.

2 Ⓓ The passage points out, "They additionally hinder the passage of fish upriver and downriver and prevent people from using rivers for recreational purposes. Despite most dams having fish ladders, not all fish are capable of navigating them, so they die in large numbers." However, it does not state that any species go extinct in certain regions because of dams.

3 Ⓑ It is written, "In 1973, the Fort Edwards Dam was removed from the Hudson River in New York, and a major environmental disaster ensued. Behind it was a huge mass of contaminated silt containing deadly chemical poisons. The dam had trapped the silt, but after it was gone, the polluted matter flowed downriver, and it soon destroyed part of the river's ecosystem by poisoning the fish in the water."

4 ②, ④, ⑤ The summary sentence notes that dams are being removed in various ways since some of them cause harm to their rivers. This thought is best described in answer choices ②, ④, and ⑤. Answer choices ① and ③ are minor points, so they are incorrect. Answer choice ⑥ contains incorrect information, so it is also wrong.

Vocabulary

- **accumulate** = to gather; to collect
- **ecosystem** = the interacting of the organic and inorganic elements in a certain environment
- **reservoir** = an artificial lake created by a dam
- **rebound** = to come back; to return to one's original state

iBT Practice Test   p. 46

Answers

PASSAGE 1

1 Ⓒ	2 Ⓒ	3 Ⓐ	4 Ⓐ	5 Ⓑ
6 Ⓐ	7 Ⓑ, Ⓒ	8 Ⓐ	9 **4**	
10 ①, ②, ④				

PASSAGE 2

11 Ⓑ	12 Ⓒ	13 Ⓐ	14 Ⓒ	15 Ⓑ
16 Ⓓ	17 Ⓒ	18 Ⓒ	19 **2**	
20 ①, ③, ④				

PASSAGE 1

Answer Explanations

1 Factual Information Question

Ⓒ It is written, "Across their enormous empire, they constructed roads, amphitheaters, aqueducts, and numerous other structures, and the cities they founded were often the predecessors of modern ones."

2 Vocabulary Question

Ⓒ When Roman cities such as Rome developed in a haphazard manner, they developed in a random way.

3 Sentence Simplification Question

Ⓐ The sentence points out that Roman soldiers frequently made camps that later became urban centers during the Roman Republic and Roman Empire. This thought is best expressed by the sentence in answer choice Ⓐ.

6

4 Vocabulary Question

Ⓐ When the streets were of a uniform width, they were all the exact width.

5 Negative Factual Information Question

Ⓑ There is no mention in the paragraph of the types of weaponry which were used by soldiers to defend the cities.

6 Inference Question

Ⓐ It is written, "The blocks of *insulae* were the equivalent of modern-day urban neighborhoods, and the majority of the common people—the plebeians—lived in them. An *insula* lacked indoor water and sewage facilities, so its residents had to carry their water from nearby wells and cart their sewage to various dumping points. A larger type of home, known as a *domus*, was where wealthy individuals lived. They always resided in separate areas from the poorer citizens." Since plebeians lived in *insulae* while wealthy individuals lived in *domi*, the author implies that a *domus* had living facilities that were superior to those in an *insula*.

7 Factual Information Question

Ⓑ, Ⓒ About the forum, the passage notes, "The forum in each city was always the primary center of commerce and politics and was therefore constantly busy."

8 Reference Question

Ⓐ The "this" that was a building necessary to keep urban dwellers fed and happy was the *horreum*.

9 Insert Text Question

■ The sentence before the fourth square reads, "The basilicas served as places for people to engage in legal and business dealings, and the circuses were the equivalent of present-day horse racing tracks." The sentence to be added points out that some places were "where the Romans held chariot races and other similar forms of entertainment." This refers to the circuses, so the two sentences go well together.

10 Prose Summary Question

①, ②, ④ The summary sentence notes that Roman cities in the republic and empire years were designed similarly and contained many of the same structures. This thought is best described in answer choices ①, ②, and ④. Answer choices ③ and ⑥ are minor points, so they are incorrect answers. And answer choice ⑤ contains information that is not mentioned in the passage, so it is incorrect as well.

PASSAGE 2

Answer Explanations

11 Factual Information Question

Ⓑ It is written, "This is particularly true of the Indo-European language group. Containing more than 400 sublanguages spoken by approximately fifty percent of the world's people, this group consists of several major modern languages, including German, English, Russian, Italian, French, Spanish, and Greek."

12 Vocabulary Question

Ⓒ A groundbreaking idea is one that is revolutionary.

13 Reference Question

Ⓐ The "They" that called the source language Proto-Indo-European were scholars.

14 Vocabulary Question

Ⓒ When people intermingled with other groups, they mixed with others that they met.

15 Negative Factual Information Question

Ⓑ The author writes, "All of the languages in the Anatolian branch are dead languages today. The evidence for them existing rests on some archaeological finds with writing on stone in cuneiform. The same cannot be said for the Indo-Iranian language branch, whose many sublanguages are spoken throughout parts of Iran, Pakistan, and India."

16 Inference Question

Ⓓ In writing, "The emergence of Athens as the predominant Greek city-state in the fifth century B.C. led to its form of Greek, called Attic, to become widely used for both writing and speaking," the author implies that Attic Greek was the major dialect spoken during the time of ancient Greece.

17 Rhetorical Purpose Question

Ⓒ In the entire paragraph, the author focuses on describing the language branches that developed throughout parts of Europe.

18 Inference Question

Ⓒ The author writes, "Armenian and Albanian are distinct enough to be considered major Indo-European branches, but they are spoken in limited geographic locations and by fewer people than the other Indo-European languages," and, "The last major Indo-European language is Tocharian, a dead language." The author therefore implies that Armenian has more people that can speak its language than the Tocharian branch does.

19 Insert Text Question

2 The sentence before the second square reads, "This led people to conclude that Latin must be a daughter language of Greek since Greek civilization was highly influential on the Latin-speaking Roman civilization that later developed in Italy." The sentence to be added mentions that the notion—that Latin is a daughter language of Greek—was considered the truth for a very long time. Thus the two sentences go well together.

20 Prose Summary Question

1, 3, 4 The summary sentence notes that around half of the world's population speaks the various languages belonging to branches of the Indo-European language group. This thought is best described in answer choices 1, 3, and 4. Answer choices 2 and 5 are minor points, so they are incorrect answers. Answer choice 6 contains wrong information, so it is also incorrect.

Vocabulary Review   p. 56

Answers

A
1	emergence	2	primates
3	dialect	4	ambient
5	noteworthy		

B
1	b	2	a	3	b	4	a	5	a
6	b	7	a	8	b	9	b	10	a

Chapter 03
Factual Information

Practice with Short Passages   p. 60

A | Totem Poles

Answers 1 (A), (D)   2 (C)

Answer Explanations

1 (A), (D) About totem poles, the author writes, "An additional benefit is that they are durable so are thus less likely to rot and to fall into pieces than other trees," and, "Cedar trees are the most commonly used to make totem poles mostly because they are tall, have large diameters, have fewer branches than other trees."

2 (C) It is written, "The top section often requires extra labor since many totem poles have protrusions such as the wings of birds attached to their tops, so it is the final part to be done."

Vocabulary

- **elaborately** = ornately; decoratively
- **purview** = a range of quality, control, or concern
- **hue** = a color
- **protrusion** = something that sticks out or projects

B | The Formation of the Solar System

Answers 1 (A)   2 (A)

Answer Explanations

1 (A) The passage reads, "The nebular hypothesis posits that a huge cloud of gas and dust began collapsing on itself due to the force of gravity. As it collapsed, the conservation of angular momentum caused the gas and dust to contract further and to spin rapidly. This spinning created a central core of elements—primarily helium and hydrogen—which formed a new star, or protostar, that would eventually become the sun."

2 (A) About the frost line, the author notes, "The outer planets, on the other hand, formed into giant balls of gas since in the colder region, which is called the frost line by astronomers and which starts between Mars and Jupiter, more of the spinning disc's material survived the sun's growing heat."

Vocabulary

- **contract** = to decrease in size
- **surround** = to be completely around someone or something
- **silicate** = any mineral compound containing silicon
- **subsequently** = next; later; afterward

C | Earthquake Prediction

Answers 1 Ⓒ 2 Ⓑ

Answer Explanations

1 Ⓒ It is written, "Around the world, there are certain areas, such as Japan and the Pacific coast region of the United States, where earthquakes are frequent. These zones are located along fault lines, which mostly occur where the tectonic plates comprising the Earth's crust meet."

2 Ⓑ The author points out, "Unfortunately, using animals to predict earthquakes is unfeasible at this time as it would require an enormous effort continuously to observe and report on animal populations in earthquake zones."

Vocabulary

- **rife** = abundant; plentiful
- **seismologist** = a person who studies earthquakes
- **unfeasible** = impractical
- **precede** = to happen before something else

Mapping

❶ long-term   ❷ historical
❸ chance   ❹ behavior
❺ toads   ❻ emissions
❼ increase   ❽ months

Summary

❶ predict   ❷ seismologists
❸ frequent   ❹ Richter
❺ behavior   ❻ prior
❼ emissions   ❽ possible

Practice with Long Passages   p. 64

A | The Formation of the Global Atmosphere

Answers

1 Ⓑ   2 Ⓐ   3 Ⓓ   4 ⓵, ⓸, ⓹

Answer Explanations

1 Ⓑ When the creation of an oxygen-rich atmosphere

was forestalled, it was hindered, so it happened more slowly.

2 Ⓐ The author writes, "These algae fed off the huge amounts of carbon dioxide in the atmosphere and, through the process of photosynthesis, emitted oxygen back into the atmosphere. Over the next 300 million years, the level of oxygen in the atmosphere rose in small amounts and attained a level sufficient enough to begin combining with iron in rocks to oxidize and to produce rust."

3 Ⓓ There is no mention in the passage about ultraviolet radiation limiting the size of any of the life on the planet.

4 ⓵, ⓸, ⓹ The summary sentence points out that the Earth's atmosphere had changed several times since the creation of the planet. This thought is best described in answer choices ⓵, ⓸, and ⓹. Answer choices ⓶ and ⓷ are minor points, so they are wrong answers. And answer choice ⓺ is not mentioned in the passage, so it is also incorrect.

Vocabulary

- **methane** = a colorless, odorless, and flammable gas
- **alga** = a small aquatic organism that contains chlorophyll
- **oxidize** = to combine with oxygen
- **migrate** = to move from one place to another

B | Movies and Theatrical Performances

Answers

1 Ⓒ   2 Ⓑ   3 Ⓓ
4 Movies: ⓵, ⓶, ⓹
  Live Theatrical Performances: ⓷, ⓺

Answer Explanations

1 Ⓒ The passage reads, "Until the creating of motion pictures in the late nineteenth century, live theatrical performances were among the main ways people entertained themselves. Nowadays, the reverse is true as movie ticket sales and box office receipts far exceed those of live theater." In pointing out that "the reverse is true as movie ticket sales and box office receipts far exceed those of live theater," the author implies that plays became less popular in the twentieth century due to movies.

2 Ⓑ The author writes, "Movies cost less to attend than most live theatrical performances as tickets average around ten dollars a show while live theater is much more expensive, with tickets for Broadway productions costing hundreds of dollars or more." In doing so, the author compares the prices of tickets.

3 Ⓓ The passage notes, "Movies can be copied and viewed worldwide by millions of people at the same

time and thereby earn their producers and studios enormous returns on their investments in a relatively short amount of time."

4 Movies: [1], [2], [5]
Live Theatrical Performances: [3], [6]
About movies, the author writes, "Theatrical performances and performers also tend to be of higher quality acting wise since the performers get no second chance if they make a mistake; movie actors, on the other hand, can do as many takes as necessary to get their lines or scenes right. If theater performers flub their lines, the audience will notice, and the performance as a whole will suffer. As a result, the best actors can be found in live theatrical performances." ([1], [2]) It is also written, "Movies have several advantages over live theatrical productions, among them being of much greater scope, having casts of thousands in some cases, and using sophisticated special visual and sound effects to enhance the stories their directors want to tell." ([5]) As for live theatrical performances, the author notes, "Each time a play, opera, ballet, or musical is staged, it may utilize the same words, songs, and dance routines, but there is always something fresh for the audience to appreciate," ([3]) and, "Live theater, however, is staged on one night in one place at one time, so its earning potential is limited by the number of seats in the theater. While some more popular performances are put on in different cities at the same time, there are still far fewer simultaneous shows than movies can achieve." ([6])

Vocabulary

• enhance = to make better; to improve
• genre = a kind or type
• intense = strong with regard to feelings or emotions
• simultaneous = happening at the same time

iBT Practice Test   p. 68

Answers

PASSAGE 1

1 Ⓑ	2 Ⓓ	3 Ⓐ	4 Ⓐ	5 Ⓓ
6 Ⓐ	7 Ⓐ	8 Ⓑ	9 **3**	
10 [1], [3], [4]				

PASSAGE 2

11 Ⓓ	12 Ⓑ	13 Ⓒ	14 Ⓒ	15 Ⓑ
16 Ⓑ	17 Ⓓ	18 Ⓒ	19 **4**	
20 [1], [2], [4]				

PASSAGE 1
Answer Explanations

1 Factual Information Question

Ⓑ It is written, "These vocalizations have been at the center of some intense studies by zoologists, the primary purpose of which was to recognize when the bird learns how to make songs and calls. A secondary purpose of the studies was to understand variations in the songs and the calls that occur in different geographical regions."

2 Negative Factual Information Question

Ⓓ There is no mention in the passage about the number of different songs that the white-crowned sparrow sings.

3 Factual Information Question

Ⓐ The author notes, "The purposes of the calls vary, but the most common are alarm calls to warn others of nearby danger and harsh, rasping noises when the birds are having disputes with other males of the same species."

4 Rhetorical Purpose Question

Ⓐ About subsongs, the passage reads, "In the same set of experiments, another male chick was raised with an adult male, and, over time, the chick seemed to pick up the correct vocalizations by listening to the adult male. The chick began learning with what the zoologists called subsongs, which were weaker versions of the adult's songs. Over time, the subsongs became more similar to the adult's songs and eventually matched them perfectly."

5 Vocabulary Question

Ⓓ When the studies reinforced what zoologists already knew about other sing birds, they strengthened the knowledge that the scientists possessed.

6 Inference Question

Ⓐ It is written, "They have a short window in which to learn their songs and calls. The sparrows had to learn them in a window ranging anywhere from fifteen to fifty days after hatching." The author therefore implies that the white-crowned sparrow can learn multiple songs and calls in the first two weeks after it hatches.

7 Sentence Simplification Question

Ⓐ The sentence points out that studies conducted on sparrows in California indicated that the birds sang songs that were unique in each region. This thought is best expressed by the sentence in answer choice Ⓐ.

8 Factual Information Question

Ⓑ It is noted, "A discovery of even greater interest from the studies was that white-crowned sparrows from the same regions have distinctive dialects in their vocalizations. For example, in a study performed on three different groups in three separate regions in California, zoologists learned there was a difference in the songs from each region as well as distinctive patterns in the songs of most of the sparrows in each area. The main theory on why this occurs is that male chicks learn the songs from their fathers and, in later years, become adults and then return to the same breeding and nesting grounds."

9 Insert Text Question

3 The sentence before the third square reads, "After fifty days, males could not learn properly even if they were placed with adult males of their species." The key point in the sentence to be added is "as the birds neared two months of age, they were unable to learn their songs and calls properly." This continues the thought expressed in the sentence before the third square. Therefore, the two sentences go well together.

10 Prose Summary Question

①, ③, ④ The summary statement notes that many studies have been made on the white-crowned sparrow because of the songs and calls it vocalizes. This thought is best described in answer choices ①, ③, and ④. Answer choices ②, ⑤, and ⑥ are minor points, so they are all incorrect answers.

PASSAGE 2

Answer Explanations

11 Rhetorical Purpose Question

Ⓓ About the North Sea, the author writes, "In contrast, some areas, such as the North Sea, have higher salinity levels. In the case of the North Sea, the flowing of the Gulf Stream Current is mostly responsible for its higher salinity level." The purpose of writing that is to explain why the water in the North Sea is saltier than the water in other places.

12 Factual Information Question

Ⓑ It is written, "For instance, where fresh water enters the ocean through the onrushing flow from river mouths, the salinity level is much less."

13 Factual Information Question

Ⓒ The author points out, "The main source of ocean salinity is the inflow of fresh water containing mineral ions from land rocks. Water in the form of precipitation has an acidic quality that erodes rocks. This characteristic comes mainly from carbon dioxide in the atmosphere. When rocks erode, they release mineral ions that eventually make their way to the oceans in the form of runoff."

14 Sentence Simplification Question

Ⓒ The sentence points out that underwater volcanoes can add to the salt level of the ocean by putting mineral ions in the water as they become bigger. This thought is best expressed by the sentence in answer choice Ⓒ.

15 Rhetorical Purpose Question

Ⓑ Throughout paragraph 3, the author focuses on describing some possible reasons that the Earth's oceans became salty in nature.

16 Negative Factual Information Question

Ⓑ There is no information in the paragraph that could answer a question about who the person who came up with the theory that the Earth's oceans became full of salt billions of years in the past was.

17 Vocabulary Question

Ⓓ When there are detrimental effects to a certain action, then those effects are harmful.

18 Factual Information Question

Ⓒ The author writes, "Despite being unfit for human consumption, it is possible to purify ocean water by desalinizing it. This is usually done through a distillation process, during which seawater is heated to a certain temperature."

19 Insert Text Question

4 The sentence before the fourth square reads, "Unfortunately, humans lack this capability." The capability in the sentence is the ability to remove salt from one's body. The sentence to be added explains why humans, unlike many marine creatures never developed that ability. Thus the two sentences go well together.

20 Prose Summary Question

①, ②, ④ The summary sentence notes that many theories on how the Earth's oceans became salty exist, and the salt water has various effects on humans and animals. These thoughts are best described in answer choices ①, ②, and ④. Answer choices ③, ⑤, and ⑥ are all minor points, so they are incorrect answers.

Vocabulary Review

p. 78

Answers

A
1 oxidize
2 delicate
3 ingrained
4 seismologist
5 purview

B
| 1 a | 2 b | 3 b | 4 a | 5 b |
| 6 a | 7 b | 8 b | 9 a | 10 a |

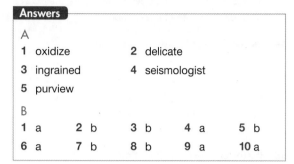

Chapter 04
Negative Factual Information

Practice with Short Passages

p. 82

A | The Migration of the Indigo Bunting

Answers   1 Ⓒ   2 Ⓐ

Answer Explanations

1 Ⓒ The passage reads, "It mostly dwells in the eastern parts of Canada and the United States during the summer breeding season." It does not breed in Mexico.

2 Ⓐ There is no mention in the paragraph of the experiments that the scientists conducted to learn about the navigational skills of the indigo bunting.

Vocabulary

• **vivid** = bright
• **brush** = dense growth of plants such as bushes and shrubs
• **approximately** = around; about
• **intensive** = focused

B | The Circulation of Water in the Oceans

Answers   1 Ⓓ   2 Ⓓ

Answer Explanations

1 Ⓓ There is no mention in the passage regarding

the reason that water does not move as fast as the wind blows.

2 Ⓓ It is not true that thermohaline circulation is more powerful deep beneath the surface rather than closer to it.

Vocabulary

• **diagonal** = slanting
• **density** = compactness
• **equilibrium** = a state of balance
• **loop** = a pattern that behaves in a circular manner

C | Herman Melville and His Work

Answers   1 Ⓑ   2 Ⓓ

Answer Explanations

1 Ⓑ There is no mention in either paragraph about what caused Herman Melville to express his feelings about religion in his works.

2 Ⓓ It is not true that Herman Melville included a great deal of religious imagery in both *Typee* and *Omoo*. The paragraph notes that there are religious topics, but it includes nothing about religious imagery.

Vocabulary

• **renowned** = famous
• **bulk** = majority
• **disillusionment** = disappointment; disenchantment
• **hypocritical** = pretending to possess virtues or beliefs one does not really have

Mapping

❶ seas   ❷ classics
❸ whaler   ❹ adventures
❺ religion   ❻ missionaries
❼ humanist   ❽ *Pierre*

Summary

❶ failed   ❷ classics
❸ reflected   ❹ influenced
❺ religion   ❻ humanist
❼ hypocritical

Practice with Long Passages

p. 86

A | Mausoleums in Ancient Societies

Answers

1 Ⓒ   2 Ⓒ   3 4
4 Greece: ⑤, ⑧, ⑨   Rome: ②, ③   China: ①, ⑥

Answer Explanations

1 Ⓒ The passage reads, "In the distant past, mausoleums were almost always built for leaders, such as the Egyptian pharaohs, for whom the pyramids were erected, but over time, it became standard to construct simpler structures for deceased individuals of more modest standing and wealth."

2 Ⓒ There is no mention in the passage of when the Romans started to bury people in mausoleums.

3 **4** The sentence before the fourth square reads, "Greek mausoleums from that time were mostly square shaped, had peaked roofs, and featured columns either in a frontal façade or surrounding the entire structure." The sentence to be added starts with "All of these styles," which refers to the characteristics of Greek mausoleums that are mentioned in the sentence before the fourth square. Therefore, the two sentences go well together.

4 Greece: ⑤, ⑧, ⑨   Rome: ②, ③   China: ①, ⑥
About Greece, the author writes, "Greek mausoleums from that time were mostly square shaped, had peaked roofs, and featured columns either in a frontal façade or surrounding the entire structure," (⑤) and, "In the initial years after they became civilized, they preferred to bury their dead in the ground with just stone markers, often with bas-relief carvings on them. Only after the conquests of Alexander the Great in the fourth century B.C. brought the Greeks into contact with more exotic cultures did their mausoleums become more elaborate." (⑧, ⑨) Regarding Rome, it is written, "The largest of these crypts even included dining rooms and kitchens for family members to use when they were making visits to honor their deceased ancestors," (②) and, "The poor were simply buried in plots while the wealthy were interred in large mausoleums, some of which can still be seen lining the roadways in places outside Rome and other urban regions." (③) As for China, the author points out, "Burial chambers could be one level or many depending upon the sizes of the structures and how many individuals were buried within them," (①) and, "The tombs of members of the imperial family tended to be inside mountains." (⑥)

Vocabulary

• **inter** = to bury
• **exotic** = foreign; unusual
• **urn** = a vase used to hold the ashes of a cremated individual
• **subterranean** = underground

B | The History of Venice

1 Ⓑ   **2** Ⓐ   **3** Ⓒ   **4** ④, ⑤, ⑥

Answer Explanations

1 Ⓑ When settlers moved to Venice in search of a refuge, they were seeking a sanctuary that would protect them from barbarian invaders.

2 Ⓐ It is noted, "With their wealth, the Venetians constructed a great city with impressive works of architecture during the city's heyday in the Middle Ages." Since Venice's heyday was in the Middle Ages, the author implies that this was the time when Venice was at the height of its greatness.

3 Ⓒ There is no mention in the paragraph about what Venice's relationships with the other European powers in the Mediterranean area were like.

4 ④, ⑤, ⑥ The summary sentence notes that Venice was at its most powerful during the Middle Ages but then lost both power and influence over time. This thought is best described in answer choices ④, ⑤, and ⑥. Answer choices ①, ②, and ③ are all minor points, so they are incorrect answers.

Vocabulary

• **ply** = to practice; to engage in
• **haven** = a safe place
• **isolated** = apart from others; alone
• **heyday** = the time when someone or something is at its peak

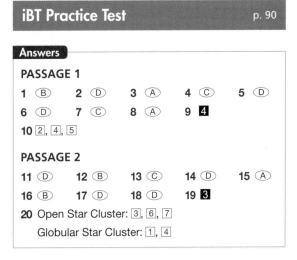

iBT Practice Test   p. 90

Answers

PASSAGE 1

1 Ⓑ	2 Ⓓ	3 Ⓐ	4 Ⓒ	5 Ⓓ
6 Ⓓ	7 Ⓒ	8 Ⓐ	9 **4**	
10 ②, ④, ⑤				

PASSAGE 2

11 Ⓓ	12 Ⓑ	13 Ⓒ	14 Ⓓ	15 Ⓐ
16 Ⓑ	17 Ⓓ	18 Ⓓ	19 **3**	
20 Open Star Cluster: ③, ⑥, ⑦				
Globular Star Cluster: ①, ④				

PASSAGE 1

Answer Explanations

1 **Factual Information Question**

Ⓑ The passage reads, "Over time, the marine

lifeforms that dwell in these places adapted to their circumstances and proved that life can survive in the harshest and most unforgiving places."

2 Rhetorical Purposes Question

Ⓓ About the angler fish, the author writes, "And some animals, such as the angler fish, use their light to draw in prey, which they attack and consume." So the author uses the angler fish as an example of an animal that can create its own light.

3 Negative Factual Information Question

Ⓐ There is no mention in the paragraph of how animals can create light from their bodies.

4 Vocabulary Question

Ⓒ Inflexible body structures are those which are rigid.

5 Factual Information Question

Ⓓ It is written, "Deep-sea creatures also lack swim bladders and other cavities which inflate and deflate because they would be easily crushed by the high pressure."

6 Negative Factual Information Question

Ⓓ According to the paragraph, it is not true that creatures consume large amounts of food to build up layers of fat in their bodies to survive the cold temperatures deep in the ocean.

7 Sentence Simplification Question

Ⓒ The sentence points out that the adaptations of some animals help them survive in their ecosystem whereas other animals would not be able to survive there. This thought is best expressed by the sentence in answer choice Ⓒ.

8 Inference Question

Ⓐ The author points out, "Deep-sea creatures frequently have slower metabolisms that enable them to survive for long periods of time on small amounts of food." It can therefore be inferred that deep-sea creatures eat less often than those animals living near the surface do.

9 Insert Text Question

◼4 The sentence before the fourth square reads, "Other lifeforms have evolved a stronger sense of smell to detect chemical scents emitted by members of the same species, which enables them to find mates." The sentence to be added mentions that some fish "sniff out prey," which indicates that the sentence is referring to some fish having "a stronger sense of smell." Therefore, the two sentences go well together.

10 Prose Summary Question

②, ④, ⑤ The summary statement notes that deep-sea creatures can survive in their extreme environment thanks to a variety of adaptations. This thought is best described in answer choices ②, ④, and ⑤. Answer choices ①, ③, and ⑥ are all minor points, so they are incorrect answers.

PASSAGE 2

Answer Explanations

11 Negative Factual Information Question

Ⓓ It is not true that star clusters are difficult for astronomers to study and to learn about as the passage reads, "Due to these characteristics, the study of star clusters is important because they can help provide astronomers with an easy way to learn more about star formation and how stars age."

12 Rhetorical Purpose Question

Ⓑ The author points out that people have known about the Pleiades cluster for thousands of years in writing, "A few nearby open star clusters can be seen from the Earth with the naked eye and have been known to humans since ancient times. Among them are the Pleiades cluster, which is around 440 light years away from the solar system, and the much closer Hyades cluster, which is only about 150 light years away."

13 Factual Information Question

Ⓒ The passage reads, "They typically form in the disk or in spiral arms of galaxies, so they are sometimes called galactic star clusters."

14 Vocabulary Question

Ⓓ When something lends credence to a theory, then belief in that theory is easy.

15 Inference Question

Ⓐ The author writes, "As they move through a galaxy, they encounter giant molecular clouds of stellar matter whose strong gravity causes individual stars to break formation with the open cluster," and, "Even though stars in an open cluster may break formation, they still move in the same direction. Astronomers call these moving groups stellar associations." The author therefore implies that stellar associations include stars in open clusters as well as stars that have broken formation with them.

16 Vocabulary Question

Ⓑ When globular star clusters have greater luminosity than open star clusters, their brightness is greater than that of open star clusters.

17 Sentence Simplification Question

Ⓓ The sentence points out that in the past, people saw globular star clusters as masses of dust but could identify individual stars in open star clusters. This thought is best expressed by the sentence in answer choice Ⓓ.

18 Factual Information Question

Ⓓ The author points out, "Observing star clusters allows astronomers to learn more about star formation, age, and luminosity. Because every star in a star cluster formed at roughly the same time from the same nebula cloud of stellar dust, the light from each star in the formation travels nearly the same distance to the Earth and reaches the planet at roughly the same time. Therefore, by observing just one star in the cluster, astronomers can utilize the readings of that single star to make inferences about the other stars in the same cluster."

19 Insert Text Question

3 The sentence before the third square reads, "It was only when the telescope was invented in the seventeenth century that astronomers became able to distinguish individual stars located in globular star clusters." The sentence to be added mentions "this," which refers to the invention of the telescope. It then provides a result of that invention, which is that people came to realize how many stars were in some clusters. Thus the two sentences go well together.

20 Fill in a Table Question

Open Star Cluster: ③, ⑥, ⑦
Globular Star Cluster: ①, ④
Regarding open star clusters, the author writes, "A few nearby open star clusters can be seen from the Earth with the naked eye and have been known to humans since ancient times. Among them are the Pleiades cluster, which is around 440 light years away from the solar system, and the much closer Hyades cluster, which is only about 150 light years away." (③) The author also writes, "They typically form in the disk or in spiral arms of galaxies, so they are sometimes called galactic star clusters," (⑥) and, "Open star clusters are normally fewer than thirty light years in diameter and include anywhere between fifty and approximately 1,000 stars." (⑦) As for globular star clusters, the author notes, "Globular star clusters are usually found close to the center of a galaxy and move around the central halo," (①) and, "Globular star clusters differ from open star clusters in several ways. They have a great deal more stars with some clusters containing millions of them."(④)

Vocabulary Review p. 100

Chapter 05
Sentence Simplification

Practice with Short Passages p. 104

A | The Archaeological Study of Pottery

Answers Ⓐ

Answer Explanations

The sentence points out that archaeologists can learn a lot about the past by studying pottery if they know where the pottery was made and where it was unearthed. This thought is best expressed by the sentence in answer choice Ⓐ.

Vocabulary

• **unearth** = to dig up; to excavate
• **durable** = long-lasting; strong
• **brittle** = easily breakable; fragile
• **fire** = to cook; to heat

B | The Origins of the Chinese Han Dynasty

Answers Ⓒ

Answer Explanations

The sentence points out that Liu Bang once worked as a lawman, but when he became afraid for his life, he fled, started a gang, and started fighting the Qin. This thought is best expressed by the sentence in answer choice Ⓒ.

C | The Mid-Atlantic Ridge

Answers   Ⓓ

Answer Explanations

The sentence points out that forces within the Earth have made islands, including Iceland, in parts of the mountain range. This thought is best expressed by the sentence in answer choice Ⓓ.

Vocabulary

• **extensive** = great in size
• **boundary** = a border
• **precise** = exact
• **credence** = believability; credibility

Mapping

❶ longest   ❷ Iceland
❸ boundary   ❹ magma
❺ Continental   ❻ oldest
❼ youngest

Summary

❶ stretches   ❷ tectonic
❸ apart   ❹ magma
❺ valley   ❻ credence
❼ Basalt   ❽ farthest

Practice with Long Passages   p. 108

A | The Origins of Oil Painting

Answers

1 Ⓓ   2 Ⓒ   3 Ⓑ   4 ①, ②, ⑥

Answer Explanations

1 Ⓓ There is no mention in the passage of how many layers of oil paints artists can apply.

2 Ⓒ The sentence points out that a twelfth-century document by the Byzantine monk Theophilus refers to making oil paints and shows that the Byzantines may have learned the technique themselves. These thoughts are best expressed by the sentence in answer choice Ⓒ.

3 Ⓑ The "They" that are uncertain precisely when and how Jan van Eyck developed oil paints are most art historians.

4 ①, ②, ⑥ The summary sentence notes that the advantages of oil paints over water-based paints and egg tempera made them popular with European artists beginning in the 1600s. This thought is best described in answer choices ①, ②, and ⑥. Answer choice ③ contains incorrect information, so it is wrong. Answer choices ④ and ⑤ are minor points, so they are incorrect as well.

Vocabulary

• **gel** = a semi-rigid solid
• **mural** = a painting done on a wall or ceiling
• **span** = to cover a certain amount of time
• **delicate** = fine; gentle

B | Friedrich Froebel and Kindergarten

Answers

1 Ⓐ   2 Ⓒ   3 Ⓐ, Ⓑ   4 ①, ②, ⑤

Answer Explanations

1 Ⓐ The sentence points out that Froebel loved being outside and that his beliefs and hometown made him believe all creatures are connected to one another. This thought is best expressed by the sentence in answer choice Ⓐ.

2 Ⓒ The author focuses on the beliefs of Johann Heinrich Pestalozzi in writing, "Fortunately for Froebel, the school at which he was employed was one of the first outside Switzerland to utilize the methods of Johann Heinrich Pestalozzi. This famed individual, who helped Switzerland become one of the first nations in Europe to achieve nearly 100% literacy, believed that children had an enormous capacity and desire to learn. His style allowed children to explore their natural curiosity rather than having them sit for hours while listening to lectures and learning by rote methods."

3 Ⓐ, Ⓑ The passage reads, "At Froebel's school, singing and dancing were used to encourage healthy activities in children. He also developed a series of geometric building blocks—today called Froebel Gifts—that the children played with and used to understand geometry and to develop spatial awareness. A third aspect of his educational style was to allow the children to work in a garden, where they could watch plants grow and learn to care for them."

4 ①, ②, ⑤ Regarding The summary sentence notes that Friedrich Froebel founded kindergarten because of his beliefs on educating children. This thought

is best described in answer choices ①, ②, and ⑤. Answer choices ③ and ④ contain information that is not mentioned in the passage, so they are incorrect. Answer choice ⑥ contains incorrect information, so it is also wrong.

Vocabulary

· **devout** = pious; sincere
· **abruptly** = suddenly; at once
· **capacity** = an ability; a capability
· **revolutionary** = new; groundbreaking; radical

iBT Practice Test   p. 112

Answers

PASSAGE 1

1 Ⓒ	2 Ⓑ	3 Ⓐ	4 Ⓑ	5 Ⓒ
6 Ⓓ	7 Ⓑ	8 Ⓑ	9 ①	
10 ①, ③, ⑥				

PASSAGE 2

11 Ⓑ	12 Ⓓ	13 Ⓐ	14 Ⓑ	15 Ⓒ
16 Ⓐ	17 Ⓒ	18 Ⓑ	19 ③	
20 ①, ⑤, ⑥				

PASSAGE 1

Answer Explanations

1 Inference Question

Ⓒ Because the author writes, "Established sometime between 1400 and 1200 B.C.," it can be inferred that precisely when the Olmec civilization was founded is unknown to historians.

2 Factual Information Question

Ⓑ It is written, "Human figures are typical representations in Olmec art and often have cleft heads, thick lips, almond-shaped eyes, and downturned mouths. Animals, especially fish and snakes, are common figures in Olmec art, but jaguars held a special place in Olmec beliefs."

3 Sentence Simplification Question

Ⓐ The sentence points out that archaeologists do not know for sure but believe the heads depict Olmec rulers that were honored by the Olmec people. This thought is best expressed by the sentence in answer choice Ⓐ.

4 Negative Factual Information Question

Ⓑ There is no mention in the paragraph of where the stone heads have been unearthed.

5 Vocabulary Question

Ⓒ A common motif is a theme.

6 Factual Information Question

Ⓓ The author declares, "On a smaller scale, the Olmecs were adept at creating tiny stone figurines, typically from jade. They were particularly skilled at making masks, also from jade. Some masks were small and might have served as decorations while others were life sized and were likely worn on people's faces during ceremonies."

7 Vocabulary Question

Ⓑ Rich hues are shades of various colors.

8 Factual Information Question

Ⓑ The passage notes, "The conclusion they have reached is that the pottery was a major trade item for the Olmecs."

9 Insert Text Question

① The sentence before the first square reads, "Among the most renowned of all Olmec art objects are the enormous stone heads that have been discovered at numerous ancient sites." The sentence to be added mentions two of the locations where the enormous heads have been found. Therefore, the two sentences go well together.

10 Prose Summary Question

①, ③, ⑥ The summary sentence notes that the Olmecs created many kinds of art that had human and animal depictions. This thought is best described in answer choices ①, ③, and ⑥. Answer choices ② and ④ are not mentioned in the passage, so they are both incorrect. Answer choice ⑤ is a minor point, so it is wrong as well.

PASSAGE 2

Answer Explanations

11 Vocabulary Question

Ⓑ When the American economy was boosted, it was greatly improved.

12 Rhetorical Purpose Question

Ⓓ In writing, "The economy was assisted by the United States' new position as a world leader. The onset of the Cold War between the U.S. and the Soviet Union resulted in an arms race as each side sought to develop massive and powerful military forces. The American government funneled enormous sums of money to its military forces, allowing them to grow to a tremendous size for a peacetime military. These funds were paid for with income tax dollars taken from the growing American workforce, which had been aided by the return to the country of millions of soldiers, many of whom entered universities paid for by the G.I. Bill," the author mentions the Cold War to show how it helped improve the post-war American economy.

13 Factual Information Question

(A) The passage reads, "These funds were paid for with income tax dollars taken from the growing American workforce, which had been aided by the return to the country of millions of soldiers, many of whom entered universities paid for by the G.I. Bill. It provided educational supplements to soldiers and allowed more people to attend universities than at any previous time in American history. University"

14 Sentence Simplification Question

(B) The sentence points out that the president signed a law that had to do with roads, and that resulted in more cars being manufactured. This thought is best expressed by the sentence in answer choice (B).

15 Inference Question

(C) The author writes, "President Eisenhower signed the Federal Aid Highway Act of 1956, which began the interstate highway building program, thereby greatly enhancing automobile production. This interstate highway system also contributed to economic growth as large parts of the nation became connected by the more than 60,000 kilometers of roads that were constructed." Because "large parts of the nation became connected," the author implies that the interstate highway system made it easier for people to drive through the country after 1956.

16 Negative Factual Information Question

(A) In paragraph 4, there is no mention of how any new construction techniques for homes made the price of housing decline.

17 Factual Information Question

(C) It is written, "One other area where the economic boom had a negative impact was on small farmers. Large numbers of farms were purchased by corporations when the food industry started expanding and becoming more streamlined. Small family-owned farms could not compete with large food corporations, so this, in turn, resulted in more people abandoning their farms to find work in urban centers."

18 Vocabulary Question

(B) When the growth of the American economy happened unabated, it was improving nonstop.

19 Insert Text Question

3 The sentence before the third square reads, "Following the war's end in 1945, Americans feared a return to poor economic conditions, but this did not happen as the economic momentum of the war carried over into peacetime." The sentence to be added provides a contrast to the thought that poor economic conditions would return as it mentions that the economy instead grew at an unprecedented rate. Thus the two sentences go well together.

20 Prose Summary Question

⑴, ⑸, ⑹ The summary sentence notes that the American economy after World War II became powerful for several reasons. This thought is best described in answer choices ⑴, ⑸, and ⑹. Answer choice ⑵ is a minor point, so it is an incorrect answer. Answer choice ⑶ contains wrong information, so it is also incorrect. And answer choice ⑷ contains information not mentioned in the passage, so it is wrong as well.

Vocabulary Review   p. 122

Answers

A
1	momentum	2	fired
3	spanned	4	funneling
5	boundary		

B
1 a	2 b	3 b	4 a	5 b
6 a	7 a	8 b	9 a	10 b

Chapter 06

Inference

Practice with Short Passages   p. 126

A | The Honeybee Waggle Dance

Answers   1 ©   2 ④

Answer Explanations

1 © The passage reads, "Honeybees dwell in hives in colonies called swarms, each of which has a queen bee and a few male drones, which are used for reproductive purposes, while the bulk of the insects are female worker bees." Then, the passage mentions that scouts are sent out to look for a new home. Since they are doing work, it can be inferred that all of the scouts are females.

2 ④ It is written, "Gradually, the most aggressive dancers win over the less forceful ones, which abandon their places around the swarm and move to the side where the most aggressive dancers are flying. Eventually, every scout winds up doing the waggle dance on the same side. At that point, the swarm follows the scouts to the new location, where they begin constructing their hive." Since all of the scouts wind up "doing the waggle dance on the same side" before they fly off to the new location, the author is implying that the honeybees must reach a consensus before they start building their new hive.

Vocabulary

- **drone** = a male bee that is stingless and makes no honey
- **waggle** = the act of moving back and forth
- **optimal** = best; ideal
- **prowess** = ability; skill

B | Interpreting Texts on Ancient Relics

Answers   1 ©   2 ④

Answer Explanations

1 © The author writes, "One solution is to utilize a key, such as the Rosetta Stone, which was discovered in Egypt in 1799. It contains an ancient Egyptian decree written in three languages,

one of which is in Egyptian hieroglyphics, an unknown language at the time of its discovery; however, another language on it is ancient Greek, which scholars understood. By comparing the text, scholars made great leaps in interpreting hieroglyphics." It can therefore be inferred that hieroglyphics is read and understood by some people today.

2 ④ The author writes, "The Rosetta Stone was mostly intact," and, "For instance, the Tel Dan Stone, a stone with ancient Hebrew inscriptions that was found in Israel in 1993, is broken in places, and large portions of text are missing." The author therefore implies that the Tel Dan Stone has less of its text intact than the Rosetta Stone does.

Vocabulary

- **complication** = something difficult, complex, or problematic
- **bias** = prejudice; hostile feelings toward a person or group
- **decipher** = to discover the meaning of
- **exacerbate** = to make worse or more difficult

C | The Roaring Twenties

Answers   1 ⑩   2 ④

Answer Explanations

1 ⑩ The passage reads, "In many ways, the Roaring Twenties was a reaction to the death and destruction of World War I (1914–1918). Following the gloom and uncertainty of the war years, people sought good lives and pleasure, which fueled a desire to spend money and to acquire the best things. A brief recession followed the war's conclusion, but economic prosperity quickly became the norm as the desire for consumer goods resulted in the mass production of automobiles, refrigerators, telephones, and other electronic products." Since there was a lot of "death and destruction" in World War I but "good lives and pleasure" as well as "economic prosperity" in the 1920s, the author implies that the Roaring Twenties was a time of relative peace in Europe and North America.

2 ④ The author points out, "During this time, women in many nations became eligible to vote and gained more freedom," so it can be inferred that many women voted for the first time in their lives during the 1920s.

Vocabulary

- **moniker** = a name
- **exemplify** = to serve as an example
- **prosperity** = wealth; affluence

• **intimate** = very personal; private

❶ decade   ❷ economic
❸ urban   ❹ jazz
❺ vote   ❻ freedom

Summary

❶ Roaring   ❷ economic
❸ economy   ❹ relocated (= moved)
❺ culture   ❻ eligible
❼ collapsed

Practice with Long Passages   p. 130

A | Pretend Play and Child Development

Answers

1 Ⓑ   2 Ⓐ   3 Ⓐ, Ⓒ
4 Fantasy Play: ③, ⑤, ⑥ Sociodramatic Play: ①, ②

Answer Explanations

1 Ⓑ There is no mention in the passage of the roles that children assume during pretend play dictating what their future careers will be.

2 Ⓐ The passage mentions, "For instance, a child might say, 'I am swimming now,' and then make swimming motions with his arms. As children age and spend more time with other children, fantasy play gradually transforms into sociodramatic play. At that point, children engage in pretend scenarios and go through them without explaining what they are doing at each stage. For example, a group of children pretending to be like pirates will act like buccaneers for a long time without having to say, 'We're pirates,' or, 'We're attacking the ship now.'" It also notes, "Children also learn what is possible and impossible as they use more realistic situations, such as playing doctor while someone pretends to be sick, when engaging in sociodramatic play." Thus it can be inferred that children doing sociodramatic play do not feel the need to state aloud what actions they are doing.

3 Ⓐ, Ⓒ The author writes, "They develop and express more positive emotions, become more thoughtful, learn to engage with others in positive ways, and understand how others feel in various situations. At the same time, they start to become able to control negative emotions such as selfishness and anger. Finally, by playing in groups, children learn that they cannot be the center of attention at all times."

4 Fantasy Play: ③, ⑤, ⑥ Sociodramatic Play: ①, ② About fantasy play, the author points out, "Fantasy play begins around the age of two, which is when children frequently enter day care and interact with their peers for the first time." (③) The author also claims that children pretend "to be superheroes saving the world from aliens or some other menace," (⑤) and the passage notes, "This play includes children verbalizing when they are pretending to do something at various stages in their activities. For instance, a child might say, 'I am swimming now,' and then make swimming motions with his arms." (⑥) As for sociodramatic play, it is written, "They partake in more real-life situations that are conceivable," (①) and, "They comprehend that the world has rules and that actions have consequences." (②)

Vocabulary

• **scenario** = an imagined sequence of events
• **peer** = an equal; a person the same status or age as another
• **psychologist** = a specialist in the study of the human mind
• **menace** = a threat

B | Plant Distribution and Plate Tectonics

Answers

1 Ⓐ   2 Ⓒ   3 Ⓒ   4 ①, ④, ⑥

Answer Explanations

1 Ⓐ When an idea is scoffed at by others, it is ridiculed by them.

2 Ⓒ The passage reads, "As an example, fossils of the fernlike plant glossopteris, which appeared roughly 300 million years ago, have been discovered in places in South Africa, Australia, South America, India, and even Antarctica." Then, the author writes, "A seed-bearing tree, glossopteris was one of the dominant plants of its era and lived on the Earth for almost fifty million years." Thus the author implies that glossopteris went extinct around 250 million years ago.

3 Ⓒ The sentence points out that cycads do not grow near the coast and that when they grow near water, their seeds are too heavy to float on it. This thought is best expressed by the sentence in answer choice Ⓒ.

4 ①, ④, ⑥ The summary sentence notes that how some plant fossils were dispersed millions of years ago has helped prove that the continents were once connected. This thought is best described in answer choices ①, ④, and ⑥. Answer choice ② has incorrect information, so it is wrong. Answer choices

③ and ⑤ are minor points, so they are incorrect answers.

Vocabulary

• **substantial** = large; considerable
• **dub** = to name
• **baffle** = to confuse
• **germinate** = to begin to grow

Answers

PASSAGE 1

1 Ⓐ	2 Ⓒ	3 Ⓓ	4 Ⓑ	5 Ⓒ
6 Ⓐ	7 Ⓑ	8 Ⓒ	9 **3**	

10 ②, ⑤, ⑥

PASSAGE 2

11 Ⓑ	12 Ⓐ	13 Ⓓ	14 Ⓑ	15 Ⓓ
16 Ⓐ	17 Ⓑ	18 Ⓓ	19 **4**	

20 ①, ③, ⑥

PASSAGE 1

Answer Explanations

1 Vocabulary Question

Ⓐ When immigrants may not assimilate into their new countries, they may not adapt to them very well.

2 Negative Factual Information Question

Ⓒ There is no mention in the passage of how immigrants can overcome the problems they face in their new countries.

3 Sentence Simplification Question

Ⓓ The sentence points out that most nations let foreigners work in them for short periods of time but make permanently working and living there much harder. This thought is best expressed by the sentence in answer choice Ⓓ.

4 Inference Question

Ⓑ The author comments, "The main reason for this is that these nations have no desire for new arrivals to become burdens on their social services. Instead, they want newcomers to be hardworking, taxpaying, and productive members of society rather than unemployed deadbeats that consume large amounts of government funding while producing little in return." The author therefore implies that many foreign governments believe a large number of potential immigrants have little of benefit to offer.

5 Rhetorical Purpose Question

Ⓒ About cancer and AIDS, the author writes, "People with serious preexisting medical problems, such as cancer and AIDS, will find it practically impossible to become permanent residents in most countries since those nations do not want sick people who will require expensive medical treatment. This is especially true for countries such as Australia, Canada, and New Zealand as well as most countries in Europe, where health care is paid for by taxes." The author therefore uses them as examples of issues that could prevent people from being allowed to immigrate to new countries.

6 Factual Information Question

Ⓐ It is written, "As a result of policies such as these, most people wishing to emigrate should possess a high level of education."

7 Vocabulary Question

Ⓑ When parents have a grasp of the local language, they have knowledge of it.

8 Factual Information Question

Ⓒ About culture shock, the author notes, "On top of all these problems is the strong likelihood that newly arrived permanent residents will suffer from culture shock. This term encompasses many things, but, in essence, it is a general negative reaction one has upon leaving one's own culture to live in another environment. Sensations such as homesickness, anxiety, depression, frustration, and fear frequently overwhelm new arrivals, who feel that they do not belong in their new land and wonder if they erred in moving to it."

9 Insert Text Question

3 The sentence before the third square reads, "This is especially true for countries such as Australia, Canada, and New Zealand as well as most countries in Europe, where health care is paid for by taxes." The sentence points out that health care in some countries is paid for by taxes. The sentence to be added begins with "And even in other countries without government-run healthcare programs." This sentence creates a contrast with the previous one, so the two go well together.

10 Prose Summary Question

②, ⑤, ⑥ The summary sentence notes that there are many issues that people who want to immigrate to new lands must deal with to become permanent residents in those places. This thought is best described in answer choices ②, ⑤, and ⑥. Answer choice ① contains information that is not mentioned in the passage. Answer choice ③ contains incorrect information. And answer choice ④ is a minor point, so none of those three choices is correct.

PASSAGE 2

Answer Explanations

11 Inference Question

Ⓑ The author writes, "Mesoamerican cultures in Mexico and Central America are renowned for their impressive architectural feats as they built enormous cities with a wide variety of structures, among them being those shaped like pyramids. What is less well known is that Native American cultures north of Mexico in North America also built pyramidlike structures of their own." In writing that, the author implies that the pyramids in North America are not as well known as those that Mesoamerican cultures made.

12 Rhetorical Purpose Question

Ⓐ The author provides the name of the place where some small pyramids have been found in writing, "Near the confluence of the Fraser and Harrison rivers and close to the city of Chilliwack, British Columbia, lies the Scowlitz archaeological site. Located there was a village belonging to the Scowlitz people, who first put roots down in that area approximately 3,000 years ago. Over time, their dead were placed in burial mounds lined with stone, covered with dirt, and built in shapes like pyramids. While these three-meter-high structures are tiny compared to Egyptian and Mesoamerican pyramids, they did serve similar functions as places of burial and worship."

13 Negative Factual Information Question

Ⓓ There is no mention in the paragraph about how archaeologists managed to discovered the dig site that was located near Chilliwack, so the question in Ⓓ is not answered.

14 Sentence Simplification Question

Ⓑ The sentence points out that historians called the city Cahokia after a local tribe even though its members said their tribe had nothing to do with the city. This thought is best expressed by the sentence in answer choice Ⓑ.

15 Factual Information Question

Ⓓ It is written, "Mounds of varying sizes were additionally a part of the Mississippi culture located in what is today the central United States. This culture originated around 500 A.D. and rose to prominence in central North America around the year 1000. Near where St. Louis is today, a magnificent city that at one point housed up to 30,000 people arose. It featured dozens of large pyramids."

16 Vocabulary Question

Ⓐ When the pyramids were erected in tiers, they were built with different levels.

17 Inference Question

Ⓑ In writing, "There is evidence that the region once featured around 120 large mounds, but only eighty remain today. The pyramids were constructed of earth and were once covered in stone, but over time, locals removed many stones for modern building projects," the author implies that some of the pyramids in Cahokia were dismantled by people living in the area after the city was abandoned.

18 Factual Information Question

Ⓓ The passage reads, "The largest pyramid around the central plaza is referred to as Monks Mound. It stands thirty meters high, covers more than five and a half hectares, and once had four stories with a flat top upon which there was a large structure that may have been a place of worship."

19 Insert Text Question

④ The sentence before the fourth square reads, "Within many of the burial mounds, they unearthed tribal artifacts and the remains of the departed." The sentence to be added refers to the tribal artifacts that were unearthed and notes how they have helped archaeologists understand more about Scowlitz culture. Thus the two sentences go well together.

20 Prose Summary Question

①, ③, ⑥ The summary sentence notes that the Scowlitz and Mississippi people in North America built pyramids. This thought is best described in answer choices ①, ③, and ⑥. Answer choices ② and ⑤ are minor points, so they are incorrect answers. Answer choice ④ contains wrong information, so it is also incorrect.

Vocabulary Review   p. 144

Answers

A
1 complications		2 confluence		
3 germinate		4 sentiment		
5 intimate				

B
1 b	2 a	3 a	4 a	5 b
6 b	7 a	8 a	9 b	10 a

Chapter 07
Rhetorical Purpose

Practice with Short Passages   p. 148

A | Poetic Justice in Literature

Answers   1 Ⓓ   2 Ⓐ

Answer Explanations

1 Ⓓ The author focuses on the events in *Oedipus Rex* that result in Oedipus receiving poetic justice.

2 Ⓐ The author mentions William Shakespeare as an author who commonly used poetic justice in writing, "The plays of William Shakespeare abound with examples of poetic justice as well."

Vocabulary

- **sympathize** = to feel compassion for
- **evoke** = to produce
- **fate** = destiny
- **usurp** = to take power by force

B | The Structure of the Human Eye

Answers   1 Ⓑ   2 Ⓓ

Answer Explanations

1 Ⓑ The author focuses on how the iris works with the pupil in the paragraph.

2 Ⓓ The author writes, "The retina is formed by sensitive photoreceptor cells called rods and cones, which form the images that a person sees through the pupil."

Vocabulary

- **intricately** = complexly
- **contract** = to become smaller
- **transparent** = admitting light; clear
- **instantaneously** = instantly; at once

C | Bird Territoriality

Answers   1 Ⓒ   2 Ⓐ

Answer Explanations

1 Ⓒ About eagles and hawks, the author notes,

"Large birds of prey, including eagles and hawks, may possess home ranges covering dozens of square kilometers."

2 Ⓐ The author comments, "Male grouses defend the small patches of ground they use for breeding displays to attract females from other males of their species."

Vocabulary

- **slack** = to be relaxed
- **transgression** = the act of trespassing
- **prominent** = noticeable
- **aggrieved** = distressed; upset

Mapping

❶ defend	❷ breeding
❸ sources	❹ compete
❺ physical	❻ warnings
❼ displays	❽ fight

Summary

❶ territory	❷ seabirds
❸ aggressive	❹ protect
❺ mates	❻ contact
❼ songs	❽ posture

Practice with Long Passages   p. 152

A | Attila the Hun

Answers

1 Ⓓ   2 Ⓒ   3 ④   4 ①, ⑤, ⑥

Answer Explanations

1 Ⓓ The passage reads, "By 443, the Hun army had marched to the walls of Constantinople, the capital of the Eastern Roman Empire, but the soldiers could not get past the prominent defenses." Since the Huns could "not get past the prominent defenses" of Constantinople, the author implies that they possessed no weapons able to breach the city's walls.

2 Ⓒ About the Battle of Chalons, the author writes, "Attila's vast host met the Romans and their Visigoth allies at the Battle of Chalons in 451. The battle ended in a stalemate but effectively terminated the Huns' invasion of Gaul."

3 ④ The sentence before the fourth square reads, "Then, in 445, Bleda died, leaving Attila as the sole ruler." The sentence to be added also focuses on the death of Bleda, so the two sentences go well together.

4 ☐1, ☐5, ☐6 The summary sentence notes that Attila the Hun successfully fought the Eastern Roman Empire and then fought against the Western Roman Empire until he died. This thought is best described in answer choices ☐1, ☐5, and ☐6. Answer choices ☐2, ☐3, and ☐4 are all minor points, so they are incorrect answers.

Vocabulary

- **brand** = to name
- **impetus** = a stimulation; a motivation
- **host** = a very large group
- **stalemate** = a tie; a situation in which neither side has an advantage over

B | The First Talkies

Answers

1 Ⓐ	2 Ⓓ	3 Ⓐ	4 ☐1, ☐3, ☐4

Answer Explanations

1 Ⓐ A problematic task is one that is challenging.

2 Ⓓ About *Don Juan*, the author points out the technology that it was the first film to make use of in writing, "He started producing short sound films for public exhibition. At the same time, other inventors successfully worked on sound on disc technology, which synchronized sounds on a record disc with the images in a film. The first major motion picture to take advantage of this system was *Don Juan*, which premiered in August 1926. It used recorded music and sound effects, yet it had no recorded dialogue, so it is usually not considered the first talkie."

3 Ⓐ There is no mention of how profitable talkies were in comparison to silent films made in the 1920s in the passage.

4 ☐1, ☐3, ☐4 The summary sentence notes that studios began making talkies when they mastered the technology needed to create them and that talkies were popular with audiences. These thoughts are best described in answer choices ☐1, ☐3, and ☐4. Answer choices ☐2 and ☐5 are minor points, so they are both incorrect. Answer choice ☐6 has incorrect information, so it is also a wrong answer.

Vocabulary

- **recite** = to repeat something from memory
- **deem** = to consider; to believe
- **premiere** = to take place for the first time; to open
- **clamor** = to call for

---

iBT Practice Test p. 156

Answers

PASSAGE 1

1 Ⓓ	2 Ⓐ	3 Ⓒ	4 Ⓓ	5 Ⓓ
6 Ⓓ	7 Ⓐ	8 Ⓑ	9 **2**	

10 Unsaturated Zone: ☐3, ☐6
Saturated Zone: ☐2, ☐5, ☐7

PASSAGE 2

11 Ⓑ	12 Ⓐ	13 Ⓒ	14 Ⓓ	15 Ⓑ
16 Ⓓ	17 Ⓑ	18 Ⓓ	19 **1**	

20 ☐3, ☐5, ☐6

PASSAGE 1

Answer Explanations

1 Factual Information Question

Ⓓ It is written, "They are both vital for agriculture and for use as sources of fresh water for animals, plants, and people."

2 Rhetorical Purpose Question

Ⓐ About sand and clay, the passage reads, "More porous rocks and soil, such as sand and clay, allow water greater movement."

3 Sentence Simplification Question

Ⓒ The sentence points out that it is believed that rivers get up to thirty percent of their water from the saturated zone while lakes drain water from it as well. This thought is best expressed by the sentence in answer choice Ⓒ.

4 Vocabulary Question

Ⓓ When the saturated zone gets depleted of water, it is exhausted of it, so it has no water.

5 Negative Factual Information Question

Ⓓ It is not true that the amount of water in the capillary fringe zone is greater than the amount of water in the unsaturated and saturated zones.

6 Rhetorical Purpose Question

Ⓓ About the Ogallala Aquifer, the author remarks, "For example, one of the largest saturated zones in the United States, the Ogallala Aquifer in the Midwest, has 170,000 wells pumping twenty trillion cubic meters of water to the surface annually. The result of this extraction has been an average drop in the depth of the water table of almost four meters in the past few decades, and there have been extreme drops of up to sixty meters in some regions in Kansas. This has led to a decline in agriculture and an increase in the cost of pumping water from the saturated zone." Thus the author focuses on the changes in the area as a result of pumping large amounts of water.

7 Factual Information Question

Ⓐ It is written, "In some places, the loss of water from the saturated zone causes the subsidence of the unsaturated zone, resulting in large depressions in the land's surface."

8 Inference Question

Ⓑ The author notes, "This has led to a decline in agriculture and an increase in the cost of pumping water up from the saturated zone," so it can be inferred that fewer crops are being grown in the areas above the Ogallala Aquifer.

9 Insert Text Question

2 The sentence before the second square reads, "In other cases, overconsumption can cause the disruption of agriculture." The sentence to be added points out that the problem of the disruption of agriculture can be affected when there is a lack of rain in the region. Therefore, the two sentences go well together.

10 Fill in a Table Question

Unsaturated Zone: ③, ⑥   Saturated Zone: ②, ⑤, ⑦

About the unsaturated zone, the author writes, "Plant root systems draw water from this zone," (③) and, "Because of the greater amount of soil and rock compared to water, water has a difficult time moving through the unsaturated zone." (⑥) As for the saturated zone, the passage reads, "The saturated zone lies beneath the unsaturated zone, and its upper level is commonly called the water table." (②) It also points out, "The human usage of water from the saturated zone can have tremendous effects on the environment as taking too much water for both agriculture and human consumption can have disastrous results," (⑤) and, "Rivers and lakes, however, tend to drain water from the saturated zone as some geologists estimate that up to thirty percent of the water in some rivers comes from the saturated zone. Finally, when humans dig wells to take water from the ground, the saturated zone gets depleted of water." (⑦)

PASSAGE 2

Answer Explanations

11 Factual Information Question

Ⓑ It is written, "The snake was first discovered on Guam in 1952 but likely arrived years earlier."

12 Vocabulary Question

Ⓐ When a snake stalks its prey, the snake hides before attacking its victim.

13 Inference Question

Ⓒ The author writes, "The snake's slender body allows it to wriggle into tight places, so it easily slithers through pipes, into pet cages, and even into tiny cracks in walls. This has caused residents of Guam to be highly vigilant in protecting their homes from invasion." The author therefore implies that the residents of Guam are concerned about the potential problems the brown tree snake may cause.

14 Rhetorical Purpose Question

Ⓓ The author suggests that the American military is responsible for the brown tree snake arriving in Guam in writing, "How and when the brown tree snake arrived on Guam remains a mystery. During World War II, the American military constructed enormous bases on islands in the south Pacific Ocean, including on Guam, and all of them were connected by sea and air transport routes. There is a high probability that the snake arrived on Guam as a stowaway on a cargo ship or airplane coming from its native range of habitation."

15 Inference Question

Ⓑ The passage notes, "This theory is given legitimacy by the fact that ship and airplane crews leaving Guam always search their vessels for the invasive species, a task which frequently results in their finding the brown tree snake hidden amongst the cargo. Despite their valiant efforts, people on other islands in the Marianas, including Tinian and Saipan, have reported sighting the snake in recent years." The author therefore implies that the brown tree snake arrived on other islands in the Marianas chain from Guam.

16 Vocabulary Question

Ⓓ When wild pigs and lizards prey upon the snake, they hunt the snake and try to catch it to eat it.

17 Sentence Simplification Question

Ⓑ The sentence points out that scientists first thought that pesticides were killing animals but then determined that it was the brown tree snake that was killing them. This thought is best expressed by the sentence in answer choice Ⓑ.

18 Factual Information Question

Ⓓ It is written, "In recent years, the brown tree snake population has declined, yet experts believe this has more to do with the dwindling food supply than human efforts as the snake has effectively reached a balance point between how many can exist on the island without there being any more food sources."

19 Insert Text Question

1 The sentence before the fourth square reads, "During World War II, the American military constructed enormous bases on islands in the south Pacific Ocean, including on Guam, and all of them were connected by sea and air transport routes." The sentence to be added points out that because the islands were connected, there was a lot of contact between them by both ships and planes. Thus the two sentences go well together.

20 Prose Summary Question

③, ⑤, ⑥ The summary sentence notes that the arrival of the brown trees snake in Guam has resulted in the snake killing many of the local animals. This thought is best described in answer choices ③, ⑤, and ⑥. Answer choice ② contains incorrect information, so it is a wrong answer. Answer choices ① and ④ are minor points, so they are also incorrect answers.

❙ Vocabulary Review   p. 166

Answers

A
1 impetus	2 evoked
3 aggrieved	4 lush
5 instantaneously	

B
1 a	2 b	3 a	4 a	5 b
6 a	7 b	8 a	9 b	10 b

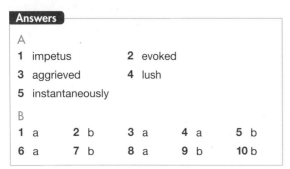

Chapter **08**

Insert Text

Practice with Short Passages   p. 170

A ❙ The Red-Billed Quelea

Answers   1 ❸   2 ❽

Answer Explanations

1 ❸ The sentence before the third square reads, "The female quelea lays anywhere from one to five eggs, which are green or blue in color and require ten to twelve days to hatch." It is about how long it takes the quelea's eggs to hatch. The sentence to be added compares that incubation period with those of other birds, so the two sentences go well together.

2 ❽ The sentence before the eighth square reads, "Millions of these small birds frequently unite to form gigantic flocks which move across the African savannah in dense, cloudlike formations and cause serious disruptions to agriculture when they swoop down on farmers' fields." The sentence to be added focuses on the "serious disruptions to agriculture" caused by the flocks of queleas, so the two sentences go well together.

Vocabulary

- **ornithologist** = a scientist who studies birds
- **beak** = the pointed end of a bird's mouth; a bird's bill
- **forage** = to search for food
- **sustenance** = food; nutrition

B ❙ Metamorphic Rocks

Answers   1 ❶   2 ❽

Answer Explanations

1 ❶ The sentence before the first square reads, "The term foliate refers to the visible colored bands present in some metamorphic rocks, so foliated rocks have these bands while non-foliated ones do not." It mentions the bands that are present in some metamorphic rocks. The sentence to be added mentions how easy or difficult the bands are to see, so the two sentences go well together.

2 ❽ The sentence before the eighth square reads, "Marble is formed from limestone, a type of sedimentary rock." The sentence to be added focuses on how marble is used, so the two sentences go well together. In addition, the sentence cannot be placed before squares ❺ or ❻ because they are about foliated rocks, which have bands. The sentence to be added mentions "The absence of bands," so this means it cannot be about the rocks mentioned in the sentences before squares ❺ and ❻.

Vocabulary

- **transform** = to change
- **collide** = to run into something
- **band** = a long strip
- **durable** = strong; long-lasting

C | John B. Watson and Behaviorism

Answers 1 ③   2 ⑥

Answers 1 ③   2 ⑥

Answer Explanations

1 ③ The sentence before the third square reads, "Watson came to his conclusions by way of his experiments with animal behavior, particularly white rats, which was the focus of his PhD dissertation." The key part of the sentence is "his PhD dissertation." The sentence to be added begins with "This work of his," which is referring to the dissertation. Thus the two sentences go well together.

2 ⑥ The sentence before the sixth square reads, "To prove his point, he conducted the Little Albert experiment, during which he subjected an eleven-month-old child named Albert to external stimulations." The sentence to be added mentions "This would prove to be an extremely controversial experiment," which refers to "the Little Albert experiment" that is included in the sentence before the sixth square. Thus the two sentences go well together.

Vocabulary

· **refine** = to improve
· **proponent** = a supporter
· **subject** = to expose a person to something
· **condition** = to put into a certain state

Mapping

❶ school
❷ 1913
❸ experiments
❹ observable
❺ predictable
❻ rage
❼ Albert
❽ conditioned

Summary

❶ behaviorism
❷ refined
❸ mind
❹ behavior
❺ (Ivan) Pavlov
❻ love
❼ experiment
❽ afraid

Practice with Long Passages   p. 174

A | The Roman Conquest of Italy

Answers

1 ⓒ   2 ⓒ   3 ②   4 ②, ④, ⑥

Answer Explanations

1 ⓒ The paragraph does not mention which part of the Italian peninsula was controlled by Rome by 396 B.C.

2 ⓒ When the city-state of Campania beseeched Rome for help, its people begged the Romans for assistance.

3 ② The sentence before the second square reads, "Pyrrhus defeated the Romans several times, but his own armies suffered great losses as well." The sentence to be added mentions the term Pyrrhic victory, which "refers to a battle that is won but in which the victor suffers heavy losses." This describes the events in the sentence before the second square, so the two sentences go well together.

4 ②, ④, ⑥ The summary statement notes that the Romans began expanding their territory after they established the Roman Republic and that it took them around 250 years to control the entire Italian peninsula. These thoughts are best described in answer choices ②, ④, and ⑥. Answer choice ① is a minor point, so it is incorrect. Answer choices ③ and ⑤ contain incorrect information, so they are also wrong answers.

Vocabulary

· **dominate** = to control; to rule over
· **setback** = a defeat
· **benevolent** = kind
· **quell** = to defeat; to put down

B | Plant Pollination

Answers

1 ⓓ   2 ⓒ   3 ④
4 Flowering Plant: ③, ⑤
  Nonflowering Plant: ④, ⑥, ⑦

Answer Explanations

1 ⓓ The passage notes, "In addition, while many nonflowering plants have both male and female parts, nature has made them unable to inbreed, so a plant cannot use the pollen from its anther to pollinate its own stigma. Therefore, these plants must spread their pollen to the female parts of other plants, which could be growing nearby or might be hundreds of meters away."

2 ⓒ The "it" that is struck by the wind is the anther.

3 ④ The sentence before the fourth square reads, "Some nonflowering plants have developed so that they contain only male parts or only female parts, making it impossible for them to inbreed, so they must be pollinated by another plant." The sentence to be added describes the gingko tree and includes the phrase "is one of these plants as there are

both male trees and females trees of that species." Therefore the two sentences go well together.

4 Flowering Plant: ③, ⑤   Nonflowering Plant: ④, ⑥, ⑦
About flowering plants, the author writes, "Insects and birds spread pollen in most flowering plants," (③) and, "Unlike flowering plants, which have sticky pollen that can cling to insects and birds." (⑤) As for nonflowering plants, the author comments, "Furthermore, the anther in nonflowering plants is very loosely attached and dangles more outside the plant compared to the anther in flowering plants. This allows the wind to strike it and then carry pollen away. Plants that receive pollen also possess enhanced abilities to catch it. The stigma hangs outside these plants so that it can lie in the path of windblown pollen, and many nonflowering plants have a feathery or netlike stigma, permitting them more easily to capture pollen." (④) It is also written, "For example, pollen is produced in the anther in far greater quantities in nonflowering plants than in flowering plants to increase the success rate of pollination," (⑥) and, "Some nonflowering plants have developed so that they contain only male parts or only female parts." (⑦)

Vocabulary

- **scented** = having a strong smell, usually pleasant in nature
- **bestow** = to give; to grant
- **enhanced** = improved
- **cling** = to hold on to; to stick to

iBT Practice Test   p. 178

Answers

PASSAGE 1

| 1 Ⓑ | 2 Ⓒ | 3 Ⓑ, Ⓓ | 4 Ⓐ | 5 Ⓑ |
| 6 Ⓒ | 7 Ⓓ | 8 Ⓐ | 9 ❷ | |

10 ①, ⑤, ⑥

PASSAGE 2

| 11 Ⓒ | 12 Ⓑ | 13 Ⓑ | 14 Ⓓ | 15 Ⓐ |
| 16 Ⓒ | 17 Ⓓ | 18 Ⓐ | 19 ❶ | |

20 ②, ④, ⑥

PASSAGE 1

Answer Explanations

1 Negative Factual Information Question

Ⓑ There is no mention in the paragraph of the manner in which the American economy changed on account of the reforms made by Woodrow Wilson.

2 Rhetorical Purpose Question

Ⓒ About the Revenue Act of 1913, the passage reads, "One of Wilson's first moves toward economic reform was the Revenue Act of 1913, which had two objectives: the lowering of tariffs and the implementing of a broad income tax on all sources of income. The income tax was intended to maintain government revenues that would be lost through the lowering of tariffs. The income tax had become law once the Sixteenth Amendment was ratified in February 1913, one month prior to Wilson taking office; however, the details of the new law had not been worked out yet. Wilson's government proposed a one-percent tax on all annual incomes exceeding $4,000 for couples and $3,000 for singles. The new law also allowed higher taxes to be levied on those earning greater incomes. And it lowered tariffs on foreign goods, which was done in the hope of increasing international trade. The immediate effectiveness of this act on the American economy is difficult to calculate though because the outbreak of World War I in 1914 tremendously upset global trade." Most of the paragraph is spent describing how it affected the economy after it was passed.

3 Factual Information Question

Ⓑ, Ⓓ It is written, "And it lowered tariffs on foreign goods," and, "Wilson's government proposed a one-percent tax on all annual incomes exceeding $4,000 for couples and $3,000 for singles. The new law also allowed higher taxes to be levied on those earning greater incomes."

4 Factual Information Question

Ⓐ The author notes, "Wilson was determined to create a federal banking system which would have a wide range of responsibilities, among them protecting people's savings and serving as the government's bank."

5 Factual Information Question

Ⓑ It is mentioned, "Therefore, the Federal Trade Commission was established in 1914 to regulate competition between companies and to protect consumers from unfair business practices."

6 Vocabulary Question

Ⓒ Loans with interest rates that were ruinous in nature were excessively high because they charged too much interest.

7 Negative Factual Information Question

Ⓓ Farmers were allowed to use their land as collateral when taking out loans, but they were taking out long-term loans, not short-term loans.

8 Rhetorical Purpose Question

Ⓐ The author writes, "Wilson attempted to reform child labor laws through the Keating-Owen Labor Act of 1916, but the Supreme Court ruled it was unconstitutional and struck it down in 1918."

9 Insert Text Question

2 The sentence before the second square reads, "The new law also allowed higher taxes to be levied on those earning greater incomes." The sentence to be added expands upon this point by noting that "individuals who made greater amounts of money than others could be forced to turn over a larger percentage of their income to the government." Therefore, the two sentences go well together.

10 Prose Summary Question

①, ⑤, ⑥ The summary statement notes that Woodrow Wilson tried to reform the American economy by passing many new laws during his two terms in office. This thought is best described in answer choices ①, ⑤, and ⑥. Answer choices ②, ③, and ④ all contain incorrect information, so they are wrong answers.

PASSAGE 2

Answer Explanations

11 Factual Information Question

Ⓒ The passage reads, "In addition, engaging in play appears to counter the belief that animals always do activities which benefit their survival while avoiding those that lessen their chances of living. Darwinian theory states that over time, species with greater survival chances will outcompete other species, yet the fact that animals play is contrary to this notion."

12 Vocabulary Question

Ⓑ When cats and dogs engage in mock fighting, they are having pretend fights with one another.

13 Factual Information Question

Ⓑ The author points out, "Researchers believe the majority of animals that engage in social play are mammals due to their more complex brains and nervous systems in comparison to other types of animals."

14 Rhetorical Purpose Question

Ⓓ The author writes, "One notion is that play starts as an aspect of parental bonding and that parents begin playing with their offspring to prepare them to engage with other young animals."

15 Negative Factual Information Question

Ⓐ There is no mention in the paragraph about what kinds of games young chimpanzees play with others.

16 Sentence Simplification Question

Ⓒ The sentence points out that scientists once thought animals played to learn safely how to become adults. This thought is best expressed by the sentence in answer choice Ⓒ.

17 Vocabulary Question

Ⓓ An inordinate amount of time is an excessive amount of time.

18 Inference Question

Ⓐ The author writes, "Despite all these theories, research proving them valid is lacking. This is partially due to the fact that it is difficult to measure play. Comparing the amount of time an animal plays and measuring the vigor the animal does it with is not a simple task." In writing that, the author implies that researchers currently lack enough information on animal play to determine if their theories are correct or not.

19 Insert Text Question

1 The sentence before the fourth square reads, "Examples include elephants sliding down muddy slopes, meerkats engaging in mass-colony melees, and cats and dogs mock fighting with their siblings while never actually clawing or biting." The sentence to be added provides an additional manner in which animals engage in play. Thus the two sentences go well together.

20 Prose Summary Question

②, ④, ⑥ The summary sentence notes that researchers recognize that playing is beneficial to animals. This thought is best described in answer choices ②, ④, and ⑥. Answer choices ①, ③, and ⑤ are all minor points, so they are incorrect.

┃ Vocabulary Review   p. 188

Answers

A
1 vigor   2 outcompete
3 ornithologist   4 setback
5 band

B
1 a   2 b   3 a   4 b   5 b
6 a   7 b   8 a   9 b   10 a

Chapter 09
Prose Summary

Practice with Short Passages — p. 192

A | The Formation of Civilization

Answers 2, 4, 5

Answer Explanations

The summary sentence notes that hunter-gatherers learned how to farm and then established permanent settlements and civilizations thousands of years ago. That thought is best described in answer choices 2, 4, and 5. Answer choice 1 is not mentioned in the passage, so it is incorrect. Answer choices 3 and 6 are minor points, so they are incorrect answers as well.

B | The Expanding Universe Theory

Answers 1, 2, 4

Answer Explanations

The summary sentence notes that the expanding universe model replaced the static universe model because of discoveries made in the twentieth century. This thought is best described in answer choices 1, 2, and 4. Answer choices 3 and 6 are minor points, so they are incorrect. Answer choice 5 has incorrect information, so it is also wrong.

C | Prions and Illness

Answers 3, 4, 5

Answer Explanations

The summary sentence notes that prions are proteins and that they cause diseases that infect the brains of their victims. This thought is best described in answer choices 3, 4, and 5. Answer choices 1, and 6 are minor points, so they are incorrect answers. Answer choice 2 is not mentioned in the passage, so it is also incorrect.

Mapping

❶ infectious
❷ cognitive
❸ nearby
❹ neurons

❺ food
❼ causes

❻ passed

Summary

❶ proteins
❸ shape
❺ Acquired
❼ sporadic

❷ kill
❹ holes
❻ Genetic

Practice with Long Passages — p. 196

A | Humanism and Renaissance Art

Answers

1 Ⓐ   2 Ⓑ   3 **1**   4 3, 4, 5

Answer Explanations

1 Ⓐ A lost art is a skill that nobody possesses any longer.

2 Ⓑ The influence of *The Last Supper* on other art produced in the Renaissance is not covered in the passage.

3 **1** The sentence before the first square reads, "The depth and lifelike aspect of Renaissance art was further enhanced by the invention of oil paints, which enabled artists to work in more detail and to include more naturalism in their works." This sentence describes the effects of oil paints, and the sentence to be added compares the types of paints that were used before oil paints became popular. Because the sentences compare the characteristics of two types of paints, they go well together.

4 3, 4, 5 The summary sentence notes that humanism had a great influence on the art of the Renaissance. This thought is best described in answer choices 3, 4, and 5. Answer choices 1 and 6 are minor points, so they are incorrect answers. Answer choice 2 is not mentioned in the passage, so it is also incorrect.

Vocabulary

• **precision** = exactness
• **enhance** = to improve; to make better
• **chiseled** = carved
• **perceive** = to think of; to consider

B | The Wilderness Road

Answers

1 Ⓓ   2 Ⓑ   3 Ⓐ   4 2, 4, 6

1 Ⓓ About Daniel Boone, the author writes, "It was not until 1775 that a route to the west was established when frontiersman Daniel Boone cut a trail from Tennessee northwest through the tail end of Virginia and then through the Cumberland Gap into Kentucky. Called the Wilderness Road, this trail, which eventually stretched more than 300 kilometers, became the principal route westward for the next fifty years." Thus the author mentions Daniel Boone to give him credit for creating the Wilderness Road.

2 Ⓑ The passage reads, "Two years later, a group of wealthy investors from North Carolina who were led by Richard Henderson, a prominent judge, formed the Transylvania Company for the purpose of making a trail into Kentucky to settle in the region and to create a new colony, which they intended to name Transylvania."

3 Ⓐ The "them" that were not deterred by attacks were Boone and his men.

4 ②, ④, ⑥ The summary sentence notes that Daniel Boone was mostly responsible for making the Wilderness Road, which enabled settlers to move into the American interior. This thought is best described in answer choices ②, ④, and ⑥. Answer choices ① and ⑤ are minor points, so they are incorrect answers. And answer choice ③ contains information that is not mentioned in the passage, so it is also incorrect.

Vocabulary

- **rugged** = rough; rocky
- **contest** = to challenge; to attempt to stop
- **abide** = to follow; to obey
- **wield** = to hold and use a tool or weapon

iBT Practice Test   p. 200

Answers

PASSAGE 1

1 Ⓒ	2 Ⓒ	3 Ⓒ	4 Ⓑ	5 Ⓒ
6 Ⓓ	7 Ⓑ	8 Ⓑ	9 ②	

10 ②, ③, ⑥

PASSAGE 2

11 Ⓐ	12 Ⓐ	13 Ⓓ	14 Ⓑ	15 Ⓒ
16 Ⓐ	17 Ⓒ	18 Ⓐ, Ⓒ	19 ②	

20 ②, ③, ④

PASSAGE 1

1 Inference Question

Ⓒ The passage reads, "When European explorers chanced upon these islands," so the author implies that the European explorers found them by accident.

2 Vocabulary Question

Ⓒ When islands are desolate, they are barren and have no life on them.

3 Sentence Simplification Question

Ⓒ The sentence points out that even though the wind cannot carry coconut seeds, they can float on water, so they are found on most of the islands in Pacific. This thought is best expressed by the sentence in answer choice Ⓒ.

4 Factual Information Question

Ⓑ The author comments, "Small seeds such as thistle seeds and the spores of ferns are lightweight enough to have been carried aloft great distances whereas heavy seeds would have had more difficulty being transported that way, especially to remote, isolated islands such as Easter Island and the Galapagos Islands. The latter group has many lichens, ferns, and mosses, which all grow from light spores, yet it has few vascular plants, which have heavier seeds."

5 Vocabulary Question

Ⓒ When birds indisputably first flew to the Pacific islands from other nearby landmass, they certainly arrived on the islands that way.

6 Negative Factual Information Question

Ⓓ It is not true that both reptiles and mammals probably swam across the ocean to the islands. About then, the passage reads, "Certainly, sea creatures such as turtles and penguins arrived by swimming to the islands. Small mammals and reptiles may have arrived by water, most likely after floating on rafts of dense vegetation which were blown out to sea during strong storms."

7 Inference Question

Ⓑ It is written, "Some animals, such as mice, were most likely stowaways on islanders' canoes." Since the mice were stowaways, it can be inferred that they were unintentionally brought to some islands by humans.

8 Factual Information Question

Ⓑ The author comments, "Unfortunately, European explorers brought many animals that caused disruptions on the islands. Dogs, rats, snakes, and cats, for instance, hunted many species of small mammals and birds to extinction."

9 Insert Text Question

2 The sentence before the second square reads, "Dogs, rats, snakes, and cats, for instance, hunted many species of small mammals and birds to extinction." The sentence to be added provides an additional example—the brown tree snake in Guam—so these two sentences go well together.

10 Prose Summary Question

②, ③, ⑥ The summary sentence notes that there were many ways that the plants and animals on the islands in the Pacific Ocean arrived at those places. This thought is best described in answer choices ②, ③, and ⑥. Answer choices ① and ④ are minor points, so they are incorrect answers. And answer choice ⑤ contains incorrect information, so it is also wrong.

PASSAGE 2

Answer Explanations

11 Vocabulary Question

Ⓐ When a place contains a wide spectrum of species of trees, it has a wide range of trees.

12 Negative Factual Information Question

Ⓐ There is no mention in the passage of the most popular species of trees found in places outside forests.

13 Sentence Simplification Question

Ⓓ The sentence points out that nobody knows how many trees outside the forest there are compared to trees in forests, and the answer will probably never be determined. This thought is best expressed by the sentence in answer choice Ⓓ.

14 Rhetorical Purpose Question

Ⓑ The author focuses on discussing a major benefit provided by trees outside the forest in writing, "Trees outside the forest additionally act as windbreaks and protect the land by preventing the wind from blowing topsoil away. This is especially important on farmland and flatland, where there are typically no nearby forests to serve as windbreaks."

15 Inference Question

Ⓒ The passage reads, "Fruit and nut trees are major sources of food for billions of people and amount to a small percentage of all trees outside the forest. In Morocco, for instance, fruit and nut trees, which include almond, palm, walnut, and fig trees, comprise twelve percent of such trees." In writing that, the author implies that people in Morocco acquire a large amount of food from trees outside

the forest.

16 Factual Information Question

Ⓐ It is written, "In Kenya, careful management and the establishment of tree-planting programs on farmland in the 1970s and 1980s means that Kenyan farmers currently produce around eighteen million cubic meters of wood for their own use and for sale as a means of supplementing their incomes."

17 Vocabulary Question

Ⓒ When trees in urban regions help regulate temperatures, they help to normalize the temperatures.

18 Factual Information Question

Ⓐ, Ⓒ The author notes, "With many regions suffering from deforestation, it is vital that people be encouraged by their governments to promote the growth of trees outside the forest. The major challenges today are to find practical ways to measure such growth and to implement national policies encouraging the planting of trees."

19 Insert Text Question

2 The sentence before the second square reads, "Alongside rivers and streams, trees outside the forest halt riverbank soil erosion and provide shade and food sources that attract fish and land animals, too." The sentence to be added explains one way that trees outside the forest that are next to rivers and streams can provide food for animals. Thus the two sentences go well together.

20 Prose Summary Question

②, ③, ④ The summary sentence notes that trees outside the forest grow in many places and help people in many ways. This thought is best described in answer choices ②, ③, and ④. Answer choice ⑥ is a minor point, so it is an incorrect answer. Answer choice ① contains information not mentioned in the passage, so it is also incorrect. And answer choice ⑤ contains wrong information, so it is incorrect as well.

| Vocabulary Review   p. 210

Answers

A
1	abide	2	dispel
3	implement	4	posits
5	aesthetic

B
| 1 a | 2 b | 3 b | 4 a | 5 b |
| 6 a | 7 a | 8 b | 9 b | 10 a |

Chapter **10**

Fill in a Table

Practice with Short Passages   p. 214

A | The Outer and Inner Cores

Answers

Outer Core: [1], [5], [7]   Inner core: [3], [4]

Answer Explanations

About the outer core, the passage reads, "The outer core is mostly comprised of liquid iron and nickel," ([1]) and, "This creates waves of convection forces, which play a major role in creating the Earth's magnetic field." ([5]) It also notes, "It starts roughly 2,900 kilometers beneath the Earth's surface, is approximately 2,200 kilometers thick, and has temperatures anywhere between 4,500 and 5,500 degrees Celsius." ([7]) As for the inner core, the author writes, "The inner core revolves eastward—the same direction as the surface—but moves at a slightly faster rate than the planet does," ([3]) and, "The inner core is also mostly iron and nickel yet is solid. It is roughly 1,220 kilometers in diameter, and its temperature reaches around 5,200 degrees Celsius. Despite this high temperature, the incredible pressure placed on the inner core by the weight of the planet prevents the atoms in the metals there from transforming from solids into liquids." ([4])

B | Carnivorous Plant Traps

Answers

Active Trap: [1], [4], [5]   Passive Trap: [2], [7]

Answer Explanations

About active traps, it is noted, "An active carnivorous plant trap involves some type of movement by the plant when capturing prey," ([1]) and, "The waterwheel plant is another carnivorous plant that catches animals in a similar manner." ([4]) The author also points out, "The leaves have small surface hairs that act as trigger mechanisms, so when an animal sucking the nectar touches them more than once in a short period of time, the trap swiftly shuts, capturing the animal." ([5]) Regarding passive traps, the author writes, "The flypaper trap, utilized by sundews and butterworts, is one such passive trap," ([2]) and, "Toxic nectar attracts

prey to the plant's rim, where the creatures, after consuming the nectar, become disoriented and fall into the hollow of the plant." ([7])

C | How Animals Regulate Their Body Temperatures

Answers

Endotherm: [2], [3], [5]   Ectotherm: [4], [7]

Answer Explanations

About endotherms, the author writes, "Nearly all mammals and birds are endotherms," ([2]) and, "In tropical zones, many endotherms sweat to make their skin cooler and to draw heat from their bodies. Most fur-bearing mammals cannot sweat well and therefore pant through the mouth, which increases the evaporation that removes heat and cools their bodies." ([3]) The author also points out, "The fur of most mammals acts like a warm coat, and mammals living in polar climates, such as polar bears, walruses, and seals, additionally have thick layers of blubber providing them with extra protection." ([5]) Regarding ectotherms, the author mentions, "Lizards and snakes lie on hot rocks to absorb heat from the sun," ([4]) and also writes, "Crocodiles and other reptiles bury themselves in cool mud to escape from the heat while fish seek warm currents to maintain their body temperatures or spend time near the surface, where sunlight heats the water." ([7])

Mapping

❶ mammals	❷ reptiles
❸ internal	❹ blubber
❺ external	❻ surface
❼ temperatures	

Summary

❶ warm	❷ endotherms
❸ ectotherms	❹ metabolizing
❺ nests	❻ sources
❼ bury	❽ internally

Practice with Long Passages   p. 218

A | The Western and Eastern Roman Empires

Answers

1 Ⓑ   2 Ⓒ   3 Ⓑ
4 Cause: [2], [4], [6]   Effect: [1], [7]

1 Ⓑ When provincial governors had a level of autonomy that practically made them minor emperors, they had a large amount of independence to do whatever they wanted.

2 Ⓒ The "them" that power went to the heads of some of were local military commanders.

3 Ⓑ It is written, "In the east, most people lived in cities and had hard currency, so tax collectors had an easier time, making money pour into Constantinople."

4 Cause: ②, ④, ⑥ Effect: ①, ⑦

Regarding the causes of the splitting of the Roman Empire, the author notes, "Diocletian opted to divide the empire primarily due to the unwieldiness of ruling a huge amount of territory." (②) The author also writes, "A series of conflicts in the decades prior to the split also showed the weakness of far-flung military commands as invasions by border people in the east and west were barely beaten back," (④) and, "Despite having an extensive network of roads and secure shipping lanes, communications were terribly slow. Messages from Rome could take weeks to reach their destinations." (⑥) As for the effects of the splitting of the Roman Empire, it is mentioned, "Hence it was natural that the Greek language and Greek customs replaced the Latin language and Roman customs in the Eastern Roman Empire," (①) and, "The end result was a rich, stable Eastern Roman Empire that withstood multiple invasions for a millennium and a poor, unstable Western Roman Empire that succumbed to invasion fewer than two centuries after the split." (⑦)

Vocabulary

- **unwieldiness** = awkwardness
- **far-flung** = distant
- **usurp** = to take over as a ruler, often by force
- **subordinate** = lower in status or power

B | Different Types of Stars

Answers

1 Ⓑ   2 Ⓓ   3 Ⓓ

4 Main Sequence Star: ①, ④, ⑥   Giant Star: ②, ⑦
White Dwarf Star: ③, ⑨

1 Ⓑ The sentence points out that even though stars look similar, there are actually many kinds of stars that have unique characteristics. This thought is best expressed by the sentence in answer choice Ⓑ.

2 Ⓓ The passage reads, "Main sequence stars are roughly the same size of the sun but can have up to six times its luminosity." In this sentence, since main sequence stars "can have up to six times" the luminosity of the sun, the author implies that the sun is much less bright than some other main sequence stars are.

3 Ⓓ About Betelgeuse, the author remarks, "Most dying main sequence stars become red giant stars, like the star Betelgeuse, although some become blue giant stars."

4 Main Sequence Star: ①, ④, ⑥   Giant Star: ②, ⑦
White Dwarf Star: ③, ⑨

About main sequence stars, the author writes, "Main sequence stars, of which the Earth's sun is one, constitute the vast majority of stars in the universe," (①) and, "Main sequence stars are roughly the same size of the sun but can have up to six times its luminosity, and their surface temperatures average around 3,500 to 7,500 degrees Kelvin. Most main sequence stars are neither very large nor hot though. Instead, they are red dwarf stars, which are smaller and much cooler than the sun and are not even visible to the naked eye from the Earth." (④, ⑥) As for giant stars, the author notes, "Giant stars can be gargantuan in scale, with some being more than 1,000 times the size of the sun," (②) and, "As gravity contracts these stars, their last remaining inner shell of hydrogen ignites and causes their rapid expansion, pushing them to giant size." (⑦) Regarding white dwarf stars, the author points out that they are "among the hottest stars in the universe" (③) and writes, "At that point, some stars explode into supernovas, yet many fail to do so as their outer layers simply dissipate into space and form planetary nebulae while gravity collapses their inner layers and leaves a dense core of material that astronomers call a white dwarf." (⑨)

Vocabulary

- **constitute** = to make up; to comprise
- **infinite** = without ending; countless
- **ignite** = to catch on fire
- **remnant** = something remaining from a larger object

PASSAGE 1

Answer Explanations

1 Sentence Simplification Question

Ⓑ The sentence points out that the understory lies beneath the canopy and has vegetation that is shorter and less thick since it gets little sunlight. This thought is best expressed by the sentence in answer choice Ⓑ.

2 Negative Factual Information Question

Ⓐ It is not true that the rainforest floor has the most vegetation. In fact, the passage reads, "Finally, there is the rainforest floor, where hardly any plant life grows due to the absence of sunlight."

3 Inference Question

Ⓒ The author writes, "Finally, there is the rainforest floor, where hardly any plant life grows due to the absence of sunlight. This is where the largest mammals and reptiles, including tigers and crocodiles, live." Since the largest predators live on the rainforest floor, it can be inferred that animals living in the emergent layer and canopy are safe from them.

4 Rhetorical Purpose Question

Ⓐ The author focuses on the way that the toucan uses its physical adaptations to get food when writing about the bird.

5 Vocabulary Question

Ⓐ When the toucan latches onto branches very tightly, it grasps them.

6 Factual Information Question

Ⓑ, Ⓒ About the jaguar, the passage reads, "It has developed powerful jaws that can kill prey with a single bite and has strong legs and sharp claws that let it climb trees to reach prey attempting to stay high above the ground to avoid predators. Two

additional adaptations are its padded paws, which permit the jaguar to walk silently through the jungle to sneak up on its prey, and its fur pattern, which provides it with camouflage while hunting."

7 Vocabulary Question

Ⓑ Because the jaguar has enhanced vision, it has excellent sight so can see very well.

8 Factual Information Question

Ⓓ The passage reads, "Most species of snakes can also sense body heat, so they can slither up to prey and attack it without warning."

9 Insert Text Question

③ The sentence before the third square reads, "Others, however, have brightly colored skin that warns predators to avoid them." The sentence to be added focuses on how predators can see the animals due to their vivid colors, so the two sentences go together.

10 Fill in a Table Question

Predator: ②, ⑥, ⑦   Prey: ①, ⑤

About predators, it is written, "Predators have adapted to the camouflage employed by prey animals by hunting at night," (②) and "Two additional adaptations are its padded paws, which permit the jaguar to walk silently to sneak up on its prey." (⑥) The author also writes, "Most species of snakes can also sense body heat, so they can slither up to prey and attack it without warning, and they can easily climb trees to seek food at most layers in the rainforest, too." (⑦) As for prey, the passage notes, "Others, however, have brightly colored skin that warns predators to avoid them," (①) and, "The sloth, for example, hides in trees and hardly moves, preventing predators from sighting it." (⑤)

PASSAGE 2

Answer Explanations

11 Sentence Simplification Question

Ⓐ The sentence points out that there are five different ocean layers animals live in and that oceanographers have identified the different characteristics of each of them. This thought is best expressed by the sentence in answer choice Ⓐ.

12 Rhetorical Purpose Question

Ⓑ The author points out that the world's coral reefs are places in the epipelagic zone that are teeming with life in writing, "In addition, the world's coral reefs, which serve as special ecological regions where myriad marine life dwells, are found in the epipelagic zone."

13 Inference Question

Ⓐ In writing, "One reason for the teeming diversity of life is the abundance of phytoplankton, which serves as a nutrition source for countless marine organisms. As smaller species consume phytoplankton, they, in turn, are food sources for larger species," the author implies that the existence of phytoplankton is of great importance to the animals in the epipelagic zone.

14 Factual Information Question

Ⓒ The author writes, "Many creatures also migrate to the upper epipelagic zone to consume food at night and then descend deeper during daylight hours."

15 Vocabulary Question

Ⓐ When animals have serrated teeth, their teeth are jagged in appearance.

16 Factual Information Question

Ⓑ The passage reads, "Others survive on marine snow, the particles of decaying dead organisms that sink from the upper layers," and, "Many creatures in this region feed on marine snow."

17 Vocabulary Question

Ⓓ Things that are hallmarks of a certain region are features, or characteristics, of it.

18 Negative Factual Information Question

Ⓑ There is no mention in the paragraph of how certain animals have adapted to be able to live in the hadalpelagic zone.

19 Insert Text Question

❸ The sentence before the third square reads, "Scientists have trouble studying many of these creatures in detail." The sentence to be added provides a contrast by pointing out that cameras and submersibles are letting scientists learn more about the creatures in that zone. Thus the two sentences go well together.

20 Fill in a Table Question

Mesopelagic Zone: ③, ⑥, ⑦
Bathypelagic Zone: ②, ⑨
Abyssopelagic Zone: ①, ⑤
Regarding the mesopelagic zone, the author writes, "The next layer is the mesopelagic zone, which extends from roughly 200 to 1,000 meters underneath the surface. Marine biologists also call it the twilight zone due to the lack of sunlight. It is a murky world, so phytoplankton cannot survive there because they depend on sunlight to produce food through photosynthesis," (③, ⑦) and, "Many creatures also migrate to the upper epipelagic zone to consume food at night and then descend deeper

during daylight hours." (⑥) As for the bathypelagic zone, the author notes, "However, some creatures, such as the bristlemouth fish and the humpbacked angler fish, dwell there. Most of the marine lifeforms in this zone have adapted to the extreme pressure by having elongated bodies with weak muscles and cartilage skeletons that bend but do not break under the pressure." (②, ⑨) And concerning the abyssopelagic zone, the author points out, "Most species in this zone, including various types of shellfish, eels, (①) and octopuses, live near the ocean floor," and, "Oceanographers estimate that more than eighty percent of the world's ocean waters comprise this zone." (⑤)

Vocabulary Review   p. 232

Answers

A
1 subordinate   2 straddles
3 Extreme   4 flux
5 infinite

B
1 b   2 a   3 b   4 a   5 b
6 b   7 a   8 b   9 a   10 b

Actual Test

Answers

PASSAGE 1

1	Ⓒ	2	Ⓐ	3	Ⓓ	4	Ⓑ	5	Ⓑ
6	Ⓒ	7	Ⓓ	8	Ⓑ	9	**4**		

10 Cause: ②, ④   Effect: ①, ③, ⑤

PASSAGE 2

11	Ⓑ	12	Ⓑ	13	Ⓒ	14	Ⓐ	15	Ⓐ
16	Ⓐ	17	Ⓓ	18	Ⓑ	19	**2**		

20 ①, ②, ⑥

PASSAGE 3

21	Ⓒ	22	Ⓑ	23	Ⓒ	24	Ⓐ	25	Ⓑ
26	Ⓐ	27	Ⓓ	28	Ⓑ, Ⓒ	29	**4**		

30 ③, ④, ⑥

PASSAGE 1
p. 235

Answer Explanations

1 Negative Factual Information Question

Ⓒ There is no mention in the paragraph of the negotiations regarding taxes that the British held with the Americans.

2 Rhetorical Purpose Question

Ⓐ About the Molasses Act of 1733, the author points out how the American colonists evaded following it by writing, "Under the Molasses Act of 1733, colonists had to pay a duty of six pence per gallon of molasses. Yet customs officials routinely accepted bribes of around one and a half pence per gallon and permitted the molasses to be shipped untaxed."

3 Factual Information Question

Ⓓ The passage reads, "Under the Molasses Act of 1733, colonists had to pay a duty of six pence per gallon of molasses. Yet customs officials routinely accepted bribes of around one and a half pence per gallon and permitted the molasses to be shipped untaxed. The Sugar Act actually reduced the duty to three pence."

4 Vocabulary Question

Ⓑ When it was mandated that that many documents the colonists used, especially those related to legal affairs and publishing, could only be written on paper with a crown revenue stamp on it, it means that the colonists were required to use paper with a crown revenue stamp on it.

5 Factual Information Question

Ⓑ It is written, "Regarding this as a direct form of taxation, the colonists protested the act so vigorously that it was repealed in 1766."

6 Rhetorical Purpose Question

Ⓒ About the Boston Tea Party, the author writes, "Among the most famous reactions to this law happened on the night of December 16, 1773. American colonists dressed as Indians stormed on board British ships in Boston Harbor and cast their cargoes of tea into the water in what came to be known as the Boston Tea Party."

7 Factual Information Question

Ⓓ The author points out, "The opposite perceptions each side had of the role of the colonists in the British Empire were the root cause of the difficulties between the opposing sides."

8 Inference Question

Ⓑ The passage reads, "But by the 1760s, the American colonies had existed for nearly 150 years and had attained a high level of autonomy." In noting that the American colonies had attained a high level of autonomy, the author implies that the colonists were used to the British government letting them run most of their own affairs.

9 Insert Text Question

4 The sentence before the fourth square reads, "American colonists dressed as Indians stormed on board British ships in Boston Harbor and cast their cargoes of tea into the water in what came to be known as the Boston Tea Party." The sentence to be added mentions the actions of the colonists, which refers to the events of the Boston Tea Party. Thus the two sentences go well together.

10 Fill in a Table Question

Cause: ②, ④   Effect: ①, ③, ⑤

Regarding the causes of the tax laws passed by the British, the author writes, "When the French and Indian War concluded in 1763, the result was an overwhelming British victory over the French that resulted in the losers being driven from most of their North American colonies. The British government, for its part, was left deeply in debt." (②, ④) As for the effects of the tax laws passed by the British, it is written, "Among the most famous reactions to this law happened on the night of December 16, 1773. American colonists dressed as Indians stormed on board British ships in Boston Harbor and cast their cargoes of tea into the water in what came to be known as the Boston Tea Party." (①) The author also notes that there were "extensive American boycotts of British goods," (③) and it is written, "The colonists protested the act so vigorously that it was repealed in 1766." (⑤)

PASSAGE 2   p. 244

Answer Explanations

11 Sentence Simplification Question

Ⓑ The sentence points out that Darwin observed various plants and animals on his journey, and his observations helped him conclude that they evolved over time to survive better. This thought is best expressed by the sentence in answer choice Ⓑ.

12 Factual Information Question

Ⓑ The author comments, "The *Beagle* was a ten-gun naval sloop—a small ship by the standards of the day—and was equipped for long exploratory expeditions with its goal being to survey the coastal waters of foreign lands."

13 Factual Information Question

Ⓒ The author points out, "However, Captain Robert Fitzroy wanted a geologist onboard to examine the land since none had been present on the first voyage, so Darwin was eventually contacted to carry out those duties."

14 Negative Factual Information Question

Ⓐ There is no mention of what happened to any of the samples that Darwin collected.

15 Inference Question

Ⓐ It is written, "But his greatest find was the discrepancy in plant and animal life in places that were short distances apart from one another. For instance, the flora and fauna of the Atlantic and Pacific coasts of Panama differed a large amount despite being relatively close to each other. He further recorded the fact that the various islands of the Galapagos had similar plants and animals but that they had evolved with slight differences which helped them survive on the particular island on which they dwelled. The most famous example of this observation is the finches Darwin noticed as having different-shaped beaks, each of which was suited for the main food source on its particular island." It can therefore be inferred that Darwin thought it was strange that animals living so closely together could be so different.

16 Vocabulary Question

Ⓐ When Darwin articulated his theory, he expressed it.

17 Rhetorical Purpose Question

Ⓓ The author focuses on the relationship between Charles Darwin and Alfred Wallace when writing, "Then, in the 1850s, he learned that his ideas were similar to those of another naturalist, Alfred Wallace, who had been working in Southeast Asia for years and had come to nearly identical conclusions with Darwin. Once they made contact, in 1858, the two men collaborated on a paper discussing evolution, making it the first published mentioning of the theory. Then, fearful that Wallace would publish a book on the subject first, Darwin's friends urged him to put his work into print. The result was *On the Origin of Species* in 1859. To his credit, Wallace never felt slighted and publicly supported Darwin and his work when both came under attack."

18 Factual Information Question

Ⓑ The author points out, "Then, fearful that Wallace would publish a book on the subject first, Darwin's friends urged him to put his work into print. The result was *On the Origin of Species* in 1859."

19 Insert Text Question

❷ The sentence before the second square reads, "The ship made its first such voyage from 1826 to 1830, where it mostly conducted a hydrographic survey of the coastal waters of South America." The sentence to be added points out that the first trip the Beagle made did not bring it any fame; however, the second trip did. The sentence that follows is about the second trip the Beagle made. Thus the two sentences go well together.

20 Prose Summary Question

①, ②, ⑥ The summary sentence notes that Charles Darwin did a great deal of the research that led him to come up with the theory of evolution on the voyage of the *Beagle*. This thought is best described in answer choices ①, ②, and ⑥. Answer choice ⑤ contains incorrect information, so it is wrong. And answer choices ③ and ④ are minor points, so they are incorrect as well.

PASSAGE 3   p. 252

Answer Explanations

21 Negative Factual Information Question

Ⓒ Why some giant stars suddenly become supernovas is not explained in the paragraph.

22 Vocabulary Question

Ⓑ A counterbalancing outside force is one that is offsetting.

23 Inference Question

Ⓒ The author writes, "A star must reach a certain size—roughly four to eight times the size of the sun—to be able to form a neutron star. Stars smaller than that typically become white dwarfs when they collapse while those larger than that normally transform into black holes upon collapsing." Thus the author implies that the Earth's sun does not have the size necessary for it to become a supernova.

24 Factual Information Question

Ⓐ The author writes, "With the star's outer layers gone, nuclear fusion is no longer possible, which results in gravity having no counterbalancing outward force. Therefore, gravity acts strongly on the core and makes it extremely dense."

25 Rhetorical Purpose Question

Ⓑ The author makes a comparison in writing, "This high rotation is explained by the law of conservation of angular momentum, which points out that an object rotates at a faster rate the more it is drawn in on itself. This is similar to the way that a figure skater begins spinning faster the moment that she pulls her arms toward her body."

26 Factual Information Question

Ⓐ The passage notes, "This magnetic field is aligned along a different axis than the spinning motion of the star, so it is like a lighthouse beam rotating in space. If the star is aligned in the right way with the Earth, astronomers using radio telescope arrays can observe this spinning magnetic field. Astronomer Jocelyn Bell first observed this phenomenon in 1967, and such stars were soon called pulsars."

27 Inference Question

Ⓓ It is written, "These observations led to the discovery of more neutron stars—almost all of them pulsars—in the following decades. Some are called millisecond pulsars because of the fact that they rotate as many as 700 times per second." It can therefore be inferred that millisecond pulsars are rare neutron stars since they rotate faster than normal.

28 Factual Information Question

Ⓑ, Ⓒ The author points out, "At present, astronomers have discovered nearly 2,000 neutron stars; however, it is believed that the number of neutron stars is far greater since all of them cannot be observed from the Earth because their rotating magnetic fields are misaligned with the planet. In addition, as neutron stars age, the speed of their rotation decelerates, preventing them from being discovered as easily as more swiftly rotating neutron stars."

29 Insert Text Question

4 The sentence before the fourth square reads, "As this density grows in strength, the electrons and protons in the core's atoms are forced together to form a core of neutrons and neutrinos." The sentence to be added refers to why neutron stars got their name. Thus the two sentences go well together.

30 Prose Summary Question

3, 4, 6 The summary sentence notes that neutron stars are small, dense, and hot and that they blink because of their spinning. These thoughts are best described in answer choices 3, 4, and 6. Answer choices 1, 2, and 5 are all minor points, so they are incorrect answers.